"Procrastination is a huge source of [ ]
time, kills enjoyment of learning, and thwarts potential. You can't ignore
the problem, and nagging certainly doesn't help. Thank goodness, then,
for Ann Dolin. In her smart, practical book, she presents a method for
dealing with procrastination that will heal relationships and get your child
on track for greater achievement and happiness."

—Daniel H. Pink, author of *When* and *Drive*

"A must read for any parent who wants to help their child navigate
through academics, whether their child is struggling or not. Ann Dolin
has produced a well researched, entertaining and easy to read guide that
can finally solve the homework battle. In 25 years of clinical practice
with families, it is decidedly one of the best resources I have ever found
to facilitate immediate change in the family dynamic around academic
achievement."

—Dr. Jeff Van Meter, clinical psychologist; founder of Legacy Clinical
    Consultants

"I wish I'd had Ann Dolin's *Getting Past Procrastination* when my son's
backpack was a middle school archeological dig of the year's papers, or
when I'd stumble upon half-finished math assignments *due yesterday*
on the coffee table. If your most uttered phrase is 'Did you do your
homework?' read this book. It's full of valuable practical advice for parents
of procrastinators."

—Jen Singer, author of *You're a Good Mom (and Your Kids Aren't So
    Bad Either)*

"Procrastination gets a bad rap, but I have always believed it is a gift. We
just need to know how to invest our time and energy and be accountable
for our results. Ann has filled this book with practical strategies to invest
your attention in achieving the most important activities. Even if you are
not a parent, you will enjoy her suggestions."

—Neen James, author of *Attention Pays*

"Ann Dolin provides clear examples of behaviors that limit the effectiveness of studying, tips to build and reward better habits, and specific strategies to help children and adolescents become more independent and efficient at studying. This book is a must-read for parents who want to reduce arguments about homework, create an environment conducive to excellent study habits, and help their children demonstrate their full potential in school and beyond."

—Dr. Jennifer Park, MD, psychiatrist

"The shelves of American bookstores are lined with Business books on Time Management, Prioritizing and Organizational Skills. This phenomenon is due to the fact that these valuable skills are not taught in our schools.

Enter Ann Dolin. Her extraordinary new book, *Getting Past Procrastination*, offers teachers and parents the tools they need to teach and foster these skills with their students and children. I recommend this book without reservation.

If a student, child or grandchild of yours is not reaching potential, *Getting Past Procrastination* may hold the key to success. . . . and you might even learn some tips that help YOU be more efficient at home and at work. Everybody wins!"

—Richard D. Lavoie, M.A., M.Ed., consultant and author of *The Motivation Breakthrough: Six Secrets to Turning On the Turned-Off Child*

Getting Past
PROCRASTINATION

How to Get Your Kids
Organized, Focused, and Motivated . . .
Without Being the Bad Guy

ANN K. DOLIN

Published by CreateSpace Independent Publishing Platform

Cover and text design by Sheila Parr
Cover image © istockphoto / ThomasVogel

Publisher's Cataloging-in-Publication data is available.

Print ISBN: 978-1721938476

First Edition

Contents

Introduction

"I just don't know what else to try."

The mother who spoke these words looked like she was on the verge of tears. Her son, whom I'll call "Josh," was bright, but constantly struggling in school. Although previously a cheerful child, Josh was rapidly becoming detached and argumentative. Meanwhile, his already mediocre grades were slipping even further.

His mother had read several books on helping children like Josh, smart students who have difficulty completing assignments on time and demonstrating their abilities on tests. She had diligently tried to implement the techniques she read about, but nothing seemed to work. In fact, her efforts often appeared to make the problem worse, frustrating her son and making him even less motivated to perform well in school.

All of us want our children to succeed. Yet too often, like Josh's mother, our efforts to support them are counterproductive, aggravating our kids far more than helping them. In my own work as an educator, tutor, and a frequent speaker on these issues, I have watched countless well-meaning parents unintentionally sacrifice their relationship with their children for the goal of increasing academic achievement. Sadly, this rarely results in improved performance, but reliably leads to heartache.

Many journalists, therapists, and child development experts have observed the growing phenomenon of well-intentioned, caring parents at their wit's end with passive, unmotivated children. How can parents break this destructive cycle? To help our children take ownership of their own performance and begin to fulfill their real potential, we need to do more than implement better study techniques. We need to reexamine our priorities and the fundamental ways we relate to our children.

This book goes beyond the "how-to's" of better grades in the short term to the heart of success in academics and in life. In addition to examining how the brain works and how exceedingly common executive weaknesses can affect academic performance, we'll explore what function motivates our kids to give their best effort to each task they encounter. We will learn how we can communicate effectively with our children without frustrating them. Most importantly, we'll talk about raising independent learners and cultivating authentic confidence that will be reflected in the quality of their relationships as well as on their report cards.

And don't worry, we will also cover plenty of practical strategies for optimizing study time, creating routines and schedules that work for your child and your family, as well as for dealing with those omnipresent screens and devices. But we'll be applying these strategies in the context of strengthening your connection with and understanding of your child as a whole person. Improved performance in school will be a byproduct, not the ultimate goal.

We want our children to enjoy academic success, but we also want them to thrive in every other area of their lives.

Fortunately, when we prioritize effective communication and cultivate healthy motivation, the rest of the pieces fall into place much more easily. The strategies and information in the chapters that follow will help produce confident, independent students and—just as importantly—happier, more relaxed parents.

1

The Procrastination Puzzle

Why kids procrastinate, how parents unknowingly add insult to injury, and how to break the cycle

"I can't believe it's 8:00 and you haven't even started your homework yet!"

On a regular Tuesday night, this situation is *not* uncommon. It's about five weeks into the new school year, and although things started off well for your child, with a new set of teachers, classmates, and notebooks, you quickly find the two of you back in the same old pattern:

Come home from work.

Make dinner.

Get everyone to put their phones and iPads down for more than ten minutes so that the family can eat together.

Finish dinner, only to find out, *yet again*, that even though you *specifically* explained what homework needed to be done after school that afternoon, it hasn't made it out of the backpack and bedtime is right around the corner.

If this sounds familiar, you're not alone. Countless children frustrate their parents by putting off homework and projects and waiting until the very last *possible* minute to study for the big unit tests that determine a large chunk of their quarterly grades.

In fact, research shows that procrastination is widespread among children as young as five[1] and that by high school 87 percent of students are "self-proclaimed procrastinators."[2]

Whether they're playing outside, watching TV, spending time on social media, or just hiding in their rooms pretending to work, some kids seem to go to great lengths to avoid taking care of their basic responsibilities. And as parents, that can feel like the single most frustrating thing in the world.

So, what's our typical response?

Whether they're playing outside, watching TV, spending time on social media, or just hiding in their rooms pretending to work, some kids seem to go to great lengths to avoid taking care of their basic responsibilities.

We scold. We nag. We apply consequences and punishments.

Sometimes we lose our tempers. And sometimes we throw up our hands and just give up altogether.

"I told you to start when you got home from soccer so that you wouldn't be up late again!"

"What do we have to do to get you to finish your assignments on time? Do we have to take away your phone again?"

"Honestly, I don't know how you think you're going to get into college if you can't sit down to study for more than five minutes at a time!"

In our calmer moments, we may sit the child down and have a heart-to-heart about responsibility, and what it's going to be like in "the real world." In our weaker moments, we might compare the child to a friend or sibling who gets all of his or her assignments done early.

"Your sister always finishes her homework before dinner!"

"Danny's mom said he got straight A's last quarter. Do you think he puts off all his work until the last minute?"

But regardless of how the frustration comes through, chances are you've realized that these types of responses seem to have the *opposite* of the intended effect, leading to defiance, defeat, or complete nuclear meltdowns.

I have yet to find a child of any age who left a nagging session feeling motivated to change his or her behavior for the better. And I have yet to find a parent who feels good about nagging. At the end of the day, we may not know what else to do, but we sense this approach just *doesn't work.*

THREE KINDS OF PROCRASTINATORS

"Kyle" is in seventh grade.

In elementary school he memorized his multiplication tables in a couple of days with no problem. He reads challenging books for pleasure on the way home from soccer practice and begged for a chemistry set for Christmas. His teachers insist he has no trouble keeping up with the concepts they are teaching and often contributes to classroom discussions. So why does Kyle put off his homework until the last minute, leading to missed assignments and mediocre grades?

"Julie" is in ninth grade.

She loves English class—her teacher comments on how well her essays flow—and she is having no problems in world civilizations or biology. But math is giving her a really hard time. Her parents are puzzled because math was easy for her in elementary school. But for some reason, she struggled in algebra last year, and this year geometry feels almost impossible. She tries hard to pay attention, but her mind often wanders in class. By the time it drifts back, she has difficulty following what the teacher is talking about and will do almost anything to avoid homework based on the concepts she didn't focus on and now doesn't understand.

"Tommy" is in fifth grade.

His grades are good, but if he misses even one question on a quiz or test, he becomes almost inconsolable. He may make only one tiny mistake on his math homework, but he will insist on copying the entire page over. His mother is worried about what will happen when he goes to middle school and the workload becomes more challenging.

Kids like Kyle, Julie and Tommy often display all the signs

Regardless of how procrastination reveals itself, it's usually for a reason we can identify.

of intelligent children. They likely play a musical instrument or participate in sports. They're curious and insightful, yet they habitually procrastinate and struggle in school. *Why?*

Now before we dig any further, let's first recognize that kids procrastinate for *all sorts* of reasons, sometimes in impressively clever ways. Some just avoid tasks they don't feel like doing at the moment, but when their backs are up against the wall, they do get their work done. Other kids will actually put off homework or studying until the situation is out of control. They may stay up late the night before an assignment is due, but they will be unable to complete it to any kind of acceptable standard. Regardless of how procrastination reveals itself, it's usually for a reason we can identify.

BRIGHT BUT DISORGANIZED: THE "CRUMPLED HOMEWORK" KID

Back when I was an elementary school teacher, I started to notice certain behavior patterns among certain types of kids. And in my time working with many more students as a tutor over the years, I've had the opportunity to observe those behaviors further—up close and personal.

It seemed that when it came to procrastination, kids fell

into one of three general categories of displaying behaviors similar to Kyle, Julie, and Tommy.

A look inside Kyle's backpack offers the first clue about what is really going on. It's full of school papers, most of them badly wrinkled from being stuffed in there haphazardly throughout the day. He has a large binder to organize his work, but the only things in it are the papers his teachers gave out during the first week of school.

Bright But Disorganized Kids:

- Are cognitively capable of doing their schoolwork
- Often leave important materials at school
- Struggle to organize their rooms, backpacks, and lockers
- May complete homework but fail to turn it in
- Frequently misplace/lose possessions (coats, lunchboxes, etc.)
- Rarely have a plan for how they will get their work done

His room is no better. His desk is covered with papers. The floor is covered with clothes—some dirty and some clean. And his mother has had to buy three pairs of soccer cleats this year, because he keeps misplacing them. He often doesn't even remember he has a homework assignment in the first place, let alone where the worksheet is.

Kids like Kyle are *Bright But Disorganized.* And they, in many respects, are the most frustrating type of procrastinator— because it's clear they could do so much better, if they could just get their act together somehow.

SUBJECT STRUGGLERS: THE "SWISS CHEESE" KIDS

It would be easy to dismiss Julie's problems by saying she's just "bad at math." But in my experience, kids like Julie don't necessarily struggle with the concepts themselves. The problem instead is that because their attentions wander so easily, they struggle in the classes where each concept builds on the previous one. This often includes mathematics, math-driven sciences like physics, chemistry, and computer science, and even foreign languages. (If this kind of problem shows up in elementary school, it can even affect reading and writing.)

Here's how it happens:

If Julie's attention is somewhere else when the algebra teacher explains the idea that you "must perform the same operation on both sides of an equation for the equation to remain valid," she will likely struggle to understand almost everything the teacher explains in class after that.

Julie may be perfectly capable of learning more sophisticated ways of manipulating variables, but without understanding this key algebraic idea, she will get lost quickly and make mistakes in her work. In English or history class, by contrast, her mind can wander a bit, but she can intuitively grasp what's going on when she "comes back."

Kids like Julie are *Subject Strugglers.* They tend to

struggle in specific subjects, driven by an inability to focus during instructional time. I sometimes call them "Swiss Cheese Kids," because of the gaps in their knowledge and skills, and they're usually the most difficult to get back on track once they start to slip.

Subject Strugglers:

- May excel in some classes, but have great difficulty in others
- May understand some concepts, but struggle with others
- Often have difficulty in subjects where each new concept builds upon the last
- May be strong students until high school, when the work becomes more challenging or an instructional method doesn't match their learning style
- Frequently find their minds wandering during class
- May be quiet and withdrawn (especially girls)
- May or may not struggle to organize their possessions

ANXIOUS PERFECTIONISTS: THE "FEAR OF FAILURE" KIDS

Kids like Tommy don't necessarily have any problems paying attention or staying organized (although some do). Tommy's primary struggle is the overpowering anxiety he has about his school work.

He is *deathly* afraid of turning in work that isn't perfect, and he interprets even a minor mistake as a mark against his worth as a person or his capability as a student, instead of looking at it as an opportunity to learn.

As they continue into middle and high school, most kids like Tommy find it impossible to turn in flawless work all the time. But the thought of making a mistake is so unpleasant, they will often try to avoid the assignment for as long as possible.

Kids like Tommy become *Anxious Perfectionists*. Unlike Julie or Kyle, these kids procrastinate because they are *hyper-focused* on every single detail and are paralyzed by the idea of failure. Their emotional state is their main barrier to success, which can be tricky to navigate.

Anxious Perfectionists:

- Hate turning in work that isn't perfect
- View anything less than an A as failure
- Associate their performance on tests with their worth as a person
- May or may not have a formal anxiety diagnosis

Not all anxious procrastinators are perfectionists, however. Some children put off their work and then become paralyzed with worry. They typically feel too overwhelmed to ask for help, and parents only figure out what's really going on when they get a call from the teacher or a bad report card. We will discuss the many different kinds of school related anxiety and how to deal with them effectively in Chapter 6.

THE ANATOMY OF A PROCRASTINATOR: WHAT'S REALLY GOING ON "UNDER THE HOOD"

It's incredibly easy to assume that procrastinators—whatever their individual tendencies or foibles—are lazy, irresponsible, or apathetic. After all, many of us adults would also prefer to watch TV or take a nap instead of going to work or cleaning the house, but we are mature enough to understand that we have to take care of our responsibilities before we can relax. So, when our kids don't do what they are supposed to—even after repeated reminders—many of us understandably conclude that they just don't care about school.

Executive function, housed in the prefrontal cortex of the brain (just behind the forehead) is what governs children's ability to organize both their thoughts and their backpacks.

But there's often more to it than that. And what many (but not all) kids like Kyle, Julie, and Tommy have in common is a weakness in their *executive function.*

Executive function, housed in the prefrontal cortex of the brain (just behind the forehead) is what governs children's ability to organize both their thoughts and their backpacks. It helps them pay attention to the teacher for the entire class period, remember the assignments she gave out, and know when they are due. It can also help kids manage whatever negative emotions they are feeling about their schoolwork without being overwhelmed by them.

And while 95 percent of the brain's structure has been formed by the time children are five or six, the prefrontal cortex is not fully developed until they reach their mid-twenties.[3] Even otherwise responsible individuals in their late teens and early twenties will see improvement in their executive functioning as they age. So, in a very real sense, your child has not yet developed many of the cognitive abilities to manage information that you take for granted each day.

To give you a better sense of the role executive function plays, the *Center for the Developing Child* at Harvard University compares executive function to the *air traffic control tower* that tells each plane at the airport when it can take off and land:

> *"Executive function and self-regulation skills are the mental processes that enable us to plan, focus attention, remember instructions, and juggle multiple tasks successfully. Just as an air traffic control system at a busy airport safely manages the arrivals and departures of many aircraft on multiple runways, the brain needs this skill set to filter distractions, prioritize tasks, set and achieve goals, and control impulses."[4]*

And for millions of kids, executive function weaknesses lie at the root of procrastination,[5] making schoolwork much more frustrating than it needs to be.

THE EXECUTIVE FUNCTION TRIFECTA: WORKING MEMORY, COGNITIVE FLEXIBILITY, AND SELF-CONTROL

Scientists generally divide executive function skills into three categories: working memory, cognitive flexibility and self-control.

Working memory is like the RAM on a computer: it encompasses our ability to hold ideas and information in our heads while we are learning and thinking. When the teacher shows you how to find the prime factors of a number and then asks you to try it on your own, you use your working memory to recall what she showed you a few minutes ago and apply it to a new situation.

You also utilize working memory when you have an idea for a story in your head and put it down on paper. Children with weak working memory can often tell you what they want to say, but they have great difficulty writing it down in coherent sentences and paragraphs.

People with strong *cognitive flexibility* make great multi-taskers. They can be on a conference call while writing an email and planning the agenda for the rest of their day.

Cognitively flexible children are usually good readers, while individuals who are cognitively inflexible struggle to "switch gears" when confronted with a new task. At the most extreme, they may display symptoms of Asperger's Syndrome or Autism Spectrum Disorder.[6] Cognitively inflexible children find interruptions stressful and can have great difficulty coping with the natural distractions in a classroom full of other children.

We often think of *self-control* as a character trait, like honesty or courage, but it's important to remember that it is also a mental and emotional skill that can be practiced and improved.

Children are born making all kinds of involuntary movements and sounds. They don't decide to cry; they cry as an instinctual reaction to an empty tummy or a wet diaper. Over the coming months, they gradually gain control over their motor functions, learning to grasp that Cheerio between their thumb and forefinger, learning to crawl, then walk, then run.

For some children, this developmental process naturally progresses into control over their emotional reactions, where they direct their attention, and the ability to ignore distractions. Others may continue to struggle, humiliating their parents by having regular temper tantrums in the middle of the grocery store. And of course, most kids will fall somewhere between these two extremes.

All these components of executive function affect our ability to focus on a task, organize our possessions and our time, and regulate the negative emotions that cause many kids to want to put off schoolwork and other responsibilities.

It's important to remember that perfectly healthy, normal children will develop self-control at different rates, but they will also respond to the developmentally appropriate boundaries their parents set (or don't set) on their behavior.

So how does all of this relate to procrastination?

All these components of executive function affect our ability to focus on a task, organize our possessions and our time, and regulate the negative emotions that cause many kids to want to put off schoolwork and other responsibilities. For parents of kids like Kyle, Julie, and Tommy, understanding how these weaknesses affect them and how to help them improve is a vital first step.

EMOTION, FEAR, AND ANXIETY: A RECIPE FOR AVOIDANCE

When I was growing up in Florida, my brother and I—like so many lucky kids of our generation—spent untold joyful hours playing outside with our neighborhood friends. Our subdivision was still being built, so we would harvest plywood and cardboard from the construction sites and create incredible forts on the remaining empty lots. We played all kinds of imaginative games with toys like cap guns and bows and arrows, hallmarks of a less safety-conscious time.

There was a boy in our neighborhood, whom I'll call "Chris," who was particularly free-spirited. My mother constantly warned us to stay away from him, convinced he was troublemaker who would bring trouble on the rest of us. She wasn't exactly wrong, but she also didn't see what we saw—an adventurous kid who was loads of fun to play with.

One day, Mom's fears were validated when Chris accidentally shot me in the calf with his bow and arrow! It was a superficial wound, and he was immediately apologetic and deeply concerned for my safety. But my brother and I were far more worried about what our mother would say than about the severity of my injury.

Instead of going to her right away, we stopped the bleeding with a handful of dirty palm leaves and snuck into the kitchen to clean and bandage it up. I wore pants for a week in 90-degree weather to keep my mom from finding out what had happened!

The moral of the story?

Sometimes kids go to *great lengths* to avoid, conceal, or put off what we as parents may view as a straightforward response to the challenges they encounter at school, solely because they fear our reaction, and the negative emotions associated with the outcome. A growing body of research supports this idea.[7]

For example, imagine that the last time you went to the dentist, you had to have a root canal. Now you're due for another cleaning, but each time you think about making the appointment, your brain subconsciously reminds you of the blood curdling sound of the dentist drilling into your tooth and the excruciating pain that followed. It's not too farfetched to think that you might put off your next appointment for a month or two.

The same can go for schoolwork. For kids like Julie and Tommy, schoolwork has become an incredibly unpleasant experience. Julie's math homework feels impossible to figure out, while Tommy sees sheet after sheet of potential mistakes.

The same goes for studying for tests. You might think that kids who feel worried about a test would want to hurry up and study as much as possible. But often, because studying reminds them of the test—which they may find terrifying—they choose to avoid it for as long as possible.

Because studying reminds them of the test–which they may find terrifying– they choose to avoid it for as long as possible.

Kids like Kyle, on the other hand, tend to procrastinate because they honestly have no idea what they have to do on a given day or how much time is really passing when they're playing video games or watching YouTube videos. They look up at the clock, and they are truly shocked that it's already 8:00 when it feels like only a few minutes have passed. Then they look in the pile of papers in their backpacks and realize with horror that there's a cumulative social studies test tomorrow. And the easiest way to make that problem go away is, well . . . to put it off for as long as possible.

WHAT ABOUT ADHD?

Now before we get too much further, let's take a minute to address an extension of this topic: ADHD.

When many parents first read about the symptoms of weak executive function, they assume it is the same as ADHD, but they are not quite identical concepts. Simply put, all children with an ADHD diagnosis have weak executive function, but not all children who struggle with executive function weaknesses will be diagnosed with ADHD.

As we touched on earlier, all children have weaker executive function than adults, because their brains are less mature. This—coupled with school systems that place greater homework and studying burdens on children at younger ages than in years past—means that many normal, healthy children will procrastinate and struggle with the organizational components of school at some point.

Sometimes though, immaturity may not be the only culprit. As it stands, ADHD is a subjective diagnosis by a pediatrician or psychologist (although work is underway to make it more data-driven). The diagnosis is arrived at through a series of questionnaires filled out by both you and your child's teachers. Confirmation of ADHD does not mean you have to put your child on medication, but it does mean he or she can receive accommodations from the school, including extra time on tests and sometimes alternative ways of submitting assignments.

When should you have your child evaluated for ADHD?

All children with an ADHD diagnosis have weak executive function, but not all children who struggle with executive function weaknesses will be diagnosed with ADHD.

Generally speaking, you should seek help from your pediatrician if you suspect your child's behavior falls outside the range of normal development (e.g. a fifth-grader who flies into a rage and smashes a prized possession, or a teenager who still can't sit still in class). You should also seek a professional evaluation if the problems are chronic, if they are manifesting at home as well as at school, or if they are affecting your child's quality of life or the health of your family relationships.

Maybe your child is borderline ADHD or has executive function weaknesses that fall within the range of normal development, but she is still not responding well to your attempts to assist her. You may find it helpful to employ an executive function coach or tutor to help her learn to manage her work. One of my own sons struggled with organizing his assignments and managing his time but wasn't responding to my suggestions. After discussing options with him, I hired one of my own tutors to help him.

After meeting with the tutor, my son enthusiastically explained the strategies they had developed together. Of course, these were exactly the same strategies I had suggested to him earlier, but I certainly didn't care as long as he was able to do what he needed to do! Sometimes our kids just need to hear advice from a different person in order to really consider it and apply it to their situations.

Ultimately though, I recommend testing the approaches outlined in this book first, before taking outside action. Because in many cases, even if your child does fall into the ADHD camp, you'll see significant improvements in his or her attitudes and behavior. If you don't see improvement, or are still concerned, you can take additional steps knowing you've exhausted your other more conservative options first.

A FRESH APPROACH

In ancient Greece, within the Temple of Apollo at Delphi, there was inscribed a singular phrase, which has since been passed forward as one of the great maxims of wisdom:

γνῶθι σεαυτόν
know thyself

Our first step towards breaking the cycle of procrastination and making a fresh start with our kids is to take both a hard look at what may be going on in their lives, as well as a hard look in mirror at ourselves.

No parent wants to be the homework police, interrogating his or her kids about their assignments and doling out threats and punishments to try to get them completed.

Knowing your children will help you better diagnose what they're going through, and what may be the best approach for helping them work through it. Knowing yourself well enough to understand why you may be responding to your children in a particular way makes it much easier to temper your words and tone of voice, and any unintentional inclination to take things out on your kids.

No parent wants to be the homework police, interrogating

his or her kids about their assignments and doling out threats and punishments to try to get them completed. That's why at the end of each chapter that follows, there is a section entitled "Turn in Your Badge." This section offers specific guidance for communicating and implementing the strategies detailed in each chapter. Because all the best ideas won't help at all if we don't communicate them to our kids effectively.

We all get frustrated at times. And yes, sometimes it's justified. Because there *are* moments where the last thing you feel prepared to do is organize your children's lives when you can barely organize your own! I'm not here to judge.

But what I do want to do is provide the insight, the strategies, and the tools you need to work on procrastination and make the best of the situation in which you and your family find yourselves. And that's the goal of the chapters that lie ahead.

A QUICK RECAP

- If there are three things that will definitely not help your child's procrastination habit, they are frustration, nagging, and exasperation on your part. Our "standard approach" isn't effective.

- Most kids fit into one of three procrastination types: Bright But Disorganized, Subject Strugglers, and Anxious Perfectionists. Each has its own unique patterns.

- One common cause of difficulty with procrastination is executive function weaknesses. Some children just don't yet have the cognitive "equipment" to stay organized and on task naturally, and need structure, training, and guidance.

- Another major cause of procrastination comes from avoidance of negative emotions like anxiety and fear. Kids who have had negative experiences at school, or routinely anticipate them, can often "avoid" that pain by simply avoiding the work altogether.

- Weak executive function and ADHD are not quite the same. If you suspect your child's behavior may go beyond "normal" procrastination, consider seeking outside help in the form of a professional evaluation or an educational coach.

- Get to know your child's patterns of procrastination and attitudes towards schoolwork. Get to know your typical response to that behavior. It's the starting point for breaking the cycle.

2

The Power of Routine

Do you ever feel like your day is just a blur of activity from the time your alarm wakes you in the morning until you collapse into bed at night?

Maybe your fifth-grader missed the bus this morning, and you ended up having to drive her to school, grabbing breakfast on the way. Then after dinner, your eighth-grader suddenly asked to be taken to the craft store to get materials for a project due the next morning. And in between all that, you somehow had to figure out how to cram in work, grocery shopping, driving the swim team carpool and attending a PTA meeting.

You want to help your kids stay on top of their schoolwork, but sometimes—lots of times!—life just feels out of control.

Chaotic schedules—which all of us deal with at least some of the time—make it very easy for our kids to procrastinate with

---

You want to help your kids stay on top of their schoolwork, but sometimes—lots of times!—life just feels out of control.

---

their schoolwork. But just because our lives are complicated, doesn't mean that homework has to be put off until the last minute. As we'll talk about in a moment, **developing simple, easy-to-follow routines** that enable our children to form productive habits is our first line of defense against procrastination and disorganization. And once those routines kick in, they don't take any additional time out of our already-hectic schedules. When homework and studying become part of the rhythm of everyday life, our kids will know what is expected of them and be much less likely to put it off. This leads to less conflict, better performance, and much more enjoyable time together.

If this sounds too good to be true, don't worry. Even families with the craziest schedules can harness the power of good homework routines. It just takes a little effort and determination to get going!

HABIT FORMATION: HOW TO PUT GOOD BEHAVIOR ON AUTOPILOT

Remember learning to tie your shoes as a kid? At first, it was confusing and took forever, but soon you didn't have to think about it at all. Most habits work just like that: they're hard at first, but easy after we get used to them.

As an adult, you probably have a system for where you put your car keys. You don't really think about hanging them on the hook or putting them in the bowl, but they're always (or almost always!) there when you need them.

That is the magic of habit formation. Once a task goes on autopilot, it takes very little mental energy to perform. As parents, one of our goals is to help our children automate as many

---

Once a task goes on autopilot, it takes
very little mental energy to perform.

---

healthy behaviors as possible, including studying and homework completion.

For children with executive function weaknesses, however,
completing and turning in homework is one of the most difficult behaviors to get on autopilot. A 2016 study published
in the *Journal of School Psychology* found that children with an
ADHD diagnosis turned in an average of 12 percent fewer
assignments than their peers.[8]

In fact, the disparity in the grades of ADHD and non-
ADHD students was almost entirely due to these missing
assignments. This means a few new habits can make a huge
difference on the report card.

You've probably heard that it takes 21 days to form a new
habit, but this isn't actually true. Bad habits—like eating donuts
for breakfast every morning—are easy to form and difficult to
break. The sugar rush triggers our brains' pleasure center, and
within a few days, we'll miss it if it's not there.

But what about habits that are good for us? Researchers at
University College London determined that it can take any-
where from 18 to 254 days to automate behaviors like eating
healthier or exercising more. According to their study, these
kinds of habits took an average of 66 days to form.[9]

Every habit, whether good or bad, has three components: a
cue, the behavior itself, and a reward. The cue is what reminds
us to perform the behavior. For brushing our teeth, the cue

could be waking up in the morning or putting on our pajamas at night. The reward for brushing our teeth is that clean feeling in our mouths and of course long-term oral health.

Often, when trying to help our kids learn new habits, the **cue** ends up being some sort of verbal reminder from us. The problem with this is that our friendly reminders quickly become nagging. They also place the burden on us to keep track of everything, remember deadlines, and make sure it all gets done, instead of encouraging our kids to take ownership of their schoolwork. Whenever possible, we want to use cues like timers, electronic reminders on phones, or visual reminders like notes and calendars. (We can also tie new habits to existing routines, which we'll talk about in a minute.)

The less often we have to personally remind our children about certain behaviors, the less we have to be the "bad guy" and the more practice they get initiating those behaviors on their own. They become "self-starters," a huge step toward getting past procrastination and toward independence. Electronic and visual reminders also help us reinforce the right behaviors much more consistently, by utilizing preset systems instead of relying on our own memory!

The built-in **rewards** for the behaviors we are trying to put on autopilot tend to be long term: a good report card and ultimately the brighter future that accompanies academic success. But long-term rewards aren't always the most effective motivators. After all, we all know how the short-term fix of a piece of cake can feel way more gratifying in the moment than the long-term prospect of losing weight. In the same way, a video game or a little free time can be much more appealing than a grade our kids won't see for a few days or weeks.

Because it can be very hard for children—especially those with executive function weaknesses—to focus on big picture rewards, we want to offer them plenty of positive reinforcement for their efforts along the way. This can include lots of praise and verbal affirmation when kids stick to routines, as well as other appropriate incentives, such as star charts or stickers for younger children, or social media time for older kids.

Now, it is extremely common for kids to push back when moms and dads try to implement something new, especially during the first few days. They may theoretically agree to a time to begin their work, but once it rolls around they are suddenly too tired, have to go to the bathroom, or they have an urgent social media matter they *must* attend to. I can't tell you how many times parents have told me that something isn't working, because their children are giving them such a hard time about it. If this happens to you, don't become discouraged! You can make small concessions at first—allowing a break after they get going or permitting them to check their phones for five minutes—while continuing to stick to the basic plan.

For example, suppose you want your ninth-grader to start her homework every day at the kitchen table while you begin cooking dinner. She may initially object by asking to use her phone or take a nap. Try compromising by letting her work for five minutes and then take a break. After two or three days, try to get her to work for ten minutes and then take a break. If you can stick to this strategy for a couple of weeks, you will most likely find that she cooperates. (Since making a decree for the entire year can feel overwhelming, try to commit to a new routine for at least one quarterly marking period.)

Kids naturally resist change—like we all do—because it

takes time and energy to adjust. It probably took you a while to teach your kids to tie their shoes, but you stuck with it and they learned. Stick to your new routines, and your kids really will come around, making life much easier in the long run.

THE HOMEWORK HABIT: A CORNERSTONE ROUTINE FOR EVERY KID IN SCHOOL

"I seriously don't have that much homework!"

"It's fine, Mom! I'll get it done!"

"Can I please just finish this game first? I'll get started right after, I promise!"

If these stall tactics sound familiar, you're just like countless other families whose evenings revolve around homework. You have no control over what the teacher assigns, yet those assignments dominate the majority of your interactions with your child.

As a teacher, I saw homework as an important academic reinforcement of the skills and information I was teaching my students. But as a parent, I saw firsthand how it can easily become an unwelcome houseguest, looming ominously in the background and draining everyone's time and energy.

Fortunately, we have found that if you establish good homework habits, they can have a domino effect, positively influencing the rest of your children's school routines. The rest of this chapter will focus on establishing a reliable homework routine, but the same principles can be applied to virtually any habit, from getting up in the morning and going to bed on time, to practicing an instrument or doing chores.

The first goal of any homework routine is to circumvent these popular stall tactics and get started on time. Later in the book, we will cover many practical techniques to help kids open up those books and actually begin working. Right now, we are going to focus on setting up the right times and places for homework and sticking to them.

THE "WHEN" OF HOMEWORK

Bright but disorganized kids like Kyle (whom we met in the last chapter) are always assuring their parents that they don't have very much homework. In their minds, they really do have plenty of time before they need to get started. Meanwhile, kids like Julie and Tommy are probably avoiding homework because they find it so unpleasant. In all three cases, if we let them wait until they "feel" like doing homework, we know they will get started right before bed, or not at all!

Setting up the "when" of homework ahead of time, while making it consistent and predictable, helps our kids know what to expect. It also greatly reduces the number of times we have to poke and prod them to get going, which increases the likelihood that they'll get started without resistance, and that we'll keep our sanity.

But which times should we choose? It turns out, some segments of the day really do work better than others, but these times may vary from family to family, and kid to kid. That being said, effective homework routines need to be both consistent and flexible. Consistency enables the brain to automate activities, while flexibility allows the routine to adapt to the reality of family life.

The first step in establishing a consistent and flexible routine is to teach our kids to think about the day in terms of units (or "chunks") of time, rather than an undefined expanse of hours between school and bed. Most families' non-school hours can be divided into seven basic units:

1. Right after school
2. After a short break (usually 30 minutes)
3. Before dinner
4. Right after dinner
5. Right before bed
6. First thing in the morning
7. On the bus ride or during a study hall period

Other activities—such as sports practice, music lessons, or work—can be inserted into the daily schedule where applicable.

Effective homework routines need to be both consistent and flexible. Consistency enables the brain to automate activities, while flexibility allows the routine to adapt to the reality of family life.

Times to Avoid

As parents, many of us wish our kids would finish their homework as soon as they get home from school. This seems like the responsible thing to do: get it out of the way and then you can do the things you enjoy. Furthermore, if children are on medication for ADHD, they understandably want their kids to get homework done during that window of time when the medication is still effective.

Of course, if your child is motivated to begin his or her work right after school—whether at home, at the school library, or in an after-care program—that can work great! But otherwise, there are a few reasons it's usually best not to insist on finishing homework as soon as school is done.

First, many children need a little time to relax and unwind before they feel ready to tackle their homework. In his book *When: The Scientific Secrets of Perfect Timing,* author Dan Pink explains that most of us move through the day in three stages: a peak, a trough, and a recovery. We focus better at our peak, which tends to be around 8:00 in the morning, and we lose energy in the afternoon, before recovering a little later. For many children, this trough may fall roughly around the time they get home from school.

Especially if it has been a stressful day or they've had some negative experiences, kids may need to decompress a bit before they are ready to get started. Depending on when their lunch period is, they may also need a snack before they can productively concentrate.

Next, children in after-care may not be able to get some assignments done without help from an adult, so some homework will have to wait. And of course many students have after school sports and activities that make it impossible to get everything done as soon as school is over.

Another time that is not usually ideal for getting homework done is right before bed. There will certainly be some evenings—particularly for high schoolers—where this is unavoidable. After all, some assignments are bound to take longer than others, and some tests require extra effort to prepare for. Still, kids need time to relax before they go to sleep. Putting off studying and homework until right before bed will almost always cut into their sleep, which in turn affects their ability to stay alert in school the next day.[10]

Times to Try

So when are the best times for homework?

For children who come home right after school, it may make sense to have them start homework after a relatively short break of 30 minutes or less. However, trying to start homework after this decompression period tends to be a "prime time" for procrastination, especially if there are no reminders in place to get them going. So if this is an ideal time for your children, it's worth thinking through how you can use the strategies in this chapter to get them in the habit of starting after that initial break.

Before or after dinner can both be very productive times for kids to do homework, but of course this works best if you have an established routine that includes a regular family dinner. Naturally, if parents travel for work or students have extracurricular activities that run late, this may not be something that can happen every night. But whenever possible, try to make a family dinner part of your evening routine.[11] Not only is it a great "anchor point" for building a homework habit, it's also a positive routine overall for you and your kids.

Here are a few more guidelines to keep in mind while working to establish your homework routines:

1. Try to establish the time your kids will be doing their homework proactively, not just right before you need them to start. For example, if they are going to start working after a 30-minute break after school, you could discuss this in the morning before school, or at the beginning of the week.

2. Remember to set a timer for younger children or have older children set an alert on their phones so that the "cue" for beginning homework isn't your verbal command, but a neutral, objective reminder. Visual cues like wall calendars, white boards, and daily written schedules can work well too. (We'll talk more about strategies for organizing time in Chapter 4.)

3. Experiment with having children in aftercare commit to complete one or two simple assignments that they can do on their own before they get picked up. For example, they may have a spelling lesson each week with a very similar format, which they should be able to do without adult help. They may still have some homework to do when they get home, but they will feel good knowing their load is significantly lighter.

4. Try utilizing what I like to call "weird windows of time." For example, if your children have a short break after school, but before a sports practice or another extracurricular activity, help them plan to get a short assignment done or take time to study for a test. They won't be able to finish

everything, but they can make progress. This will mean less to do when they get home. Most schools leave the library or media center open after school for this purpose.

5. If your children spend a significant amount of time in the car traveling to and from extracurricular activities, try finding assignments or studying that they may be able to complete during the ride.

6. I suggest that you do not allow your children to watch television or play videos games before they start their homework.[12] Even with limitations, time spent with electronics leaves the brains of both children and adults less able to focus on tasks that require longer spans of attention.[13] Some parents find success restricting video games to the weekends and holidays, while others prefer to restrict them entirely. If you choose to have video games in the house, putting them off until after homework is done is the best way to set your kids up for success.

The Designated Homework Time

Another strategy you might want to try is having a **designated homework time**. The length of this time period can vary depending on the child's age. A good guideline is about 10 minutes per grade level, maxing out at about an hour.[14]

During the designated homework time, everyone in the house is pretty quiet. Younger children can color, play with Play-Doh, or be entertained outside or in a separate area. This frees older children from distractions and noise. Adults can take care of quiet tasks, like reading, working, or paying bills. If students legitimately finish their homework before the time is up, they can read for pleasure.

The designated homework time can solve several problems. First, it helps children who tend to rush through their assignments. By accepting that they are going to be working on homework for a certain period of time, they are more likely to work carefully and thoroughly. It can also help children build up a tolerance for concentrating for longer periods of time.

A designated homework time also helps kids experience the satisfaction of making progress on their work before the last minute. After all, one of the best ways to get past procrastination is to help children discover how good it feels NOT to procrastinate!

Lastly, a designated homework time can support children by showing them that everyone in the house is working quietly. They don't feel like they are missing out on anything fun, because everyone in the family is using that time to tackle important responsibilities.

Research also suggests that at least some homework should be done in relative quiet. Too much noise can stimulate the release of the stress hormone cortisol, which impairs the function of that all-important pre-frontal cortex.[15] This implies that children with executive function weaknesses may be even more vulnerable to distractions from excessive noise. So it makes sense to give them some quiet time, especially for their most challenging tasks.

The designated homework time is a wonderfully flexible tool. Depending on the family's schedule, it could be before dinner on Tuesdays and after tennis practice on Wednesdays. Try to look at your week ahead of time and determine which times you want to try. Then go over these times with your kids and set up the appropriate visual and electronic reminders.

THE "WHERE" OF HOMEWORK

"Julie, you've been up here for over an hour, and you haven't gotten anything done!"

Julie went up to her room to start her homework right after dinner, just as she and her mother had agreed. She had everything she needed to get started: her laptop, textbooks, list of assignments, and of course the brand new work station that the guy at the furniture store promised her parents would make her super-productive.

Unfortunately, after briefly checking her social media accounts, Julie noticed an adorable video of some puppies playing in the snow. That led her to several YouTube channels devoted entirely to puppy videos that no one with a heart could resist. Before she knew it, her mom poked her head in to check on her, and a typical argument followed.

Now, there are certainly plenty of times where your kids will overtly avoid doing their homework—intentionally stalling or choosing distracting activities to procrastinate. But in cases like this one, the environment where your children do their schoolwork can have significant, unintended consequences on their ability to focus and work productively. Yes, Julie was the one who made the decision to check her social media, but what if she hadn't had that option in the first place?

Here's the point: the "where" of homework can matter just as much (and sometimes more) than the "when." And paying close attention to the environment where you hope to ingrain your child's routines and habits can mean the difference between success and failure in establishing them. In my tutors' and my experience, kids will definitely be more productive in some environments than in others, and it's worth exploring which ones might work best for your family.

> The "where" of homework can matter just as much (and sometimes more) than the "when."

Locations to Avoid

Before we discuss specific homework locations, keep in mind that even though establishing routines involves repetition, kids don't actually have to do their homework in the same physical location all the time. (And they certainly don't need you to spend thousands of dollars on a sophisticated work station for their rooms!) There are certain components of productive homework environments that you should make sure are in place, but you can be flexible. In fact, mixing it up a little has some advantages, as we'll see in a minute.

That being said, there *are* some locations that typically don't work too well. Like Julie, most children are not at their most productive in their own rooms. Even if they don't have a television or other electronic devices in there, bedrooms usually offer too many distractions and not quite enough accountability. A messy room can also make it really easy to lose or misplace work.

Now you may have a child who's working successfully in her room, or a teenager who simply refuses to come out. Sometimes that's just how it goes. But younger children should be encouraged to try working in other areas of the house whenever possible.

Locations to Try

Locations like the living room couch (with a lap desk), in the recreation room, or in the family room can work fine for some kids but may not work as well for others. A great place to consider is the kitchen or dining room table. This enables you to keep a casual eye on your children's progress, while offering enough space for them to work comfortably. It can also give them the benefit of being relatively quiet without all the distractions likely to be found in other places.

It's also a great idea to have your children spend at least some time doing homework in natural light. Not only does regular exposure to sunlight improve sleep quality and overall health, it has been shown to improve students' efficiency in both math and reading.[16] This could mean studying out on the deck or in the yard, at a quiet park, or even by a large window.

Sometimes, a location outside the home actually works best. I had great success taking one of my sons to the local library where he could complete his work without distractions. Middle and high schoolers may be able to walk or take the bus to the library right after school or stay after school and work in the media center. Many kids also like working at Starbucks or other local coffee shops.

As I mentioned at the beginning of this section, don't be afraid to have your kids work in several different locations over the course of a week. Recent research indicates that varied study locations actually improve retention.[17] For example, if your child needs to learn a list of spelling or vocabulary words over the next three days, he may want to study them for the first time at the dining room table after his short break after school. The next day he might review them in the living room before dinner. After that, he might review them on the bus on the way to school. This approach will actually help him remember the words better than if he had studied them in the same location each time.

The best location for homework and studying can vary a lot from one child to another. Rather than asking kids where they think they study best, I like to encourage parents and kids to "play detective." Try different locations and ask them where they feel most productive. You will probably find that what works well for one child isn't necessarily the best option for another. That's fine! What's important is that you work with your children to find the best option for them that will result in the work getting done.

TURN IN YOUR BADGE

We've covered a lot of the benefits of healthy habits and routines, but there's a right and wrong way to introduce them to your kids. One of the biggest mistakes we've seen parents make is trying to introduce them in a time of crisis.

Imagine you've just logged onto your child's homework portal after a long day at work and you notice she got a C- on her last math test. Naturally you're upset, and you suspect her poor grade is at least partially due to her tendency to put off studying to the last minute. You know it's long past time to establish a better homework routine.

This is NOT the time to sit her down and talk about how you're going to start having a designated homework hour in the house.

If you introduce a new routine to your kids when you are feeling tired, impatient, or upset, they will probably feel like they are being punished and become defensive. Try to keep in mind that any kind of change will be an adjustment for all of you. One of the best ways to set everyone up for success is to talk about the change when you are feeling calm and positive.

Instead of laying down the law as soon as you see a bad grade, set up a time to speak to your kids later. Something as simple as "Hey, can we talk about school stuff after dinner?" or "How about if we chat about the new plan after school tomorrow?" can enable you to communicate with your kids proactively, instead of in the heat of the moment.

We want our kids to own their homework routines and learn to initiate those good behaviors on their own. One incredibly effective way to do this is by asking **powerful questions** instead of just telling them what to do (which, like adults, kids find really annoying!)

For example, most kids really hate the question, "What do you have for homework today?" They feel like they are being interrogated, and so they will often give evasive answers. Instead, try asking them something like, "What are your priorities this afternoon?

In a perfect world, your children would answer this question in great detail, explaining exactly what they have to do and the order in which they intend to do it. In reality, of course, you will probably just hear something like, "Well, I have a math test. And a social studies worksheet." But just pondering the question of priorities gets them thinking ahead. And if they can do enough of this kind of thinking on a regular basis, it will eventually develop into effective planning and prioritizing.

When putting a new routine in place, you want to open up a discussion that gives your kids buy-in and enables them to think through what they need to do. To do this, set up a time to talk when tensions are low. This not only protects your relationship with your children, but it also gives your new routine the greatest chance of success.

The right questions can also help your kids take ownership of new homework routines.

The right questions can also help your kids take ownership of new homework routines. Instead of directly reminding them about times and places, you can ask them to remind *you* what's on the schedule. (We'll talk a lot more about different kinds of powerful questions in each subsequent chapter.)

Be sure to praise your kids' effort and progress as opposed to waiting for the perfect end results. If your fifth-grader remembers to get started on his math after soccer like you agreed, tell him how pleased you are that he did the responsible thing, even if his worksheet wasn't done perfectly. If your ninth-grader sat down at the kitchen table and began her history project several days early, let her know how much you appreciate her maturity, even if she complained about how boring it was. Remember the goal is to automate these behaviors so that they take less effort. That will only come with practice.

Harnessing the power of routine is one of the most effective ways to help your kids get past procrastination. It won't happen overnight, and it will take a significant investment of effort and energy on the front end. But the long-term effects will reduce stress in your home and set your children up for success.

A QUICK RECAP

- Routines enable us to put good behaviors on autopilot. They require time and effort to get going, but once established, they help our kids become more productive while using up less mental energy.

- The "Homework Routine" is a cornerstone habit for most children. Establishing a positive and productive routine for completing homework is one of the best ways to start the process of building positive habits around their experience in school.

- Once you've established the times that kids will get started on their homework, set up visual reminders like a calendar or a written schedule where the kids can see it, as well as electronic reminders on phones and computers. These help kids become "self-starters."

- By linking homework to an existing habit like family dinnertime, your routine can be both consistent and flexible.

- A designated homework time can be a useful routine for the whole family, especially for kids who tend to rush through their work.

- Kids need some established places where they can work productively, but it doesn't need to be the same place all the time.

- Proactively communicate with kids about routines in periods of non-conflict, remembering to praise effort rather than waiting for perfect results.

3

Organization 101

Like every other year, Kyle began seventh grade with a tidy room and a perfectly organized backpack. And like every other year, his parents resolved that they would somehow help him keep them that way.

But within a month, the backpack was stuffed full of crumpled papers, broken pencils and even a moldy sandwich from the second day of school. The floor of his room was covered with clothes, soccer shorts, Legos, and comic books.

Kyle's parents put up with his messy ways in elementary school, but now that he's almost 12, they feel like they've had enough.

So they sat him down several times and talked to him about the importance of caring for his possessions and taking responsibility for his homework. Unfortunately, these talks never led to changed behavior. Instead, they almost always resulted in conflict. And the fact that Kyle's grades are suffering despite his academic capabilities only exasperates his parents more.

But Kyle's disorganization isn't just frustrating his parents. It's frustrating Kyle too.

Lots of homework assignments are getting lost in that morass of papers on the floor of his room and in the bottom of his backpack. And nothing feels worse to Kyle than taking the time to do an assignment and then not getting credit because he can't find it to turn it in.

Kyle—who was cheerful throughout elementary school—is now on the verge of really hating school. After all, what's the point of trying if you're probably going to end up with a zero anyway?

THE PRICE OF DISORGANIZATION

On paper, Kyle should be an extremely successful student. He is very bright, talented, and curious, and he has supportive, loving parents. But because he is not naturally organized, he is in great danger of performing poorly in middle school.

The struggle to get organized is beginning to negatively affect almost every part of Kyle's life. It exaggerates his weaknesses and prevents his incredible strengths from shining through. And not knowing what his homework is—or where the right materials are to complete it—is making his natural desire to procrastinate much worse.

For example, back in elementary school, Kyle sailed through math on his natural ability, often completing assignments in minutes. But now that he is in algebra, he's encountered some more difficult homework problems that he can't breeze through as quickly. Even though he's intelligent, Kyle hasn't had to develop the skills to directly deal with this discomfort. So he "sits on it." He avoids paying close attention to where he puts his homework and when it's due (out of sight, out of mind). He procrastinates, hoping that he can somehow avoid confronting the work he doesn't quite know how to do.

This is the hallmark of a "fixed mindset" (the belief that intelligence is innate and that intelligent people do not need to exert effort to learn, which we will discuss extensively in Chapter 8), and it reinforces Kyle's disorganized approach.

Kyle's inability to keep track of his tasks and materials is also creating tremendous stress for everyone in his family. His parents feel like they have to micromanage him, checking and double checking to make sure everything is getting done. And Kyle feels like Mom and Dad are constantly breathing down his neck. He doesn't understand that they're concerned not just about that one algebra assignment, but also about developing his ability to navigate the world on his own.

> Organizational skills aren't a luxury in our modern world. They are absolutely essential to long-term success.

Organizational skills aren't a luxury in our modern world. They are absolutely essential to long-term success. Even if your disorganized child is getting by with good or fair grades in high school, the struggle to keep track of things will eventually catch up with him or her. Successful high school students often have a hard time in college. Instead of weekly quizzes and worksheets, many college courses are graded only on a midterm, term paper, and a final exam. Students are responsible for pacing themselves on these larger, high-stakes assignments and for taking the initiative to get help if they need it. According to one survey, nearly half of college students said they felt "their high school did not prepare them with the organizational skills required to do well in college," while nearly 90 percent felt better organizational skills would help them improve their grades.[18]

In addition to new academic challenges, college offers students unprecedented distractions, free from parental supervision and accountability. Without strong organizational skills and self-discipline, it's all too easy to put off studying for a visit to a coffee shop or a fraternity party.

And of course, once they graduate, our children will eventually be confronted with all the normal adult responsibilities, from completing important projects for work to paying bills and doing their taxes. Yet today, many employers find that recent college graduates do not possess a multitude of skills needed for workplace success.[19] And as Anthony Carnevale and Nicole Smith of Georgetown University's *Center on Education and the Workforce* explain, "Organizational skills are the building blocks for leadership."[20]

Helping your kids develop strong organizational skills while they're still in your care sets them up to meet all these challenges. And fortunately, there are simple steps you can take to help your kids keep track of their homework, athletic equipment and sheet music, *and* reduce stress for the entire family. And you don't have to be naturally organized to implement them!

But first, it's helpful to understand a little bit more about what's going on when some kids struggle so much to get and stay organized.

WHY IS IT SO HARD FOR KIDS TO GET AND STAY ORGANIZED?

The cycle goes something like this: Kyle goes to class and has no trouble understanding what his algebra teacher is talking about. Today, it's an introduction to order of operations, and the class is learning that you multiply and divide from left to right before you add and subtract. As the class draws to a close, the teacher explains the homework assignment. Kyle is honestly convinced he will remember it, so he doesn't write it down.

Of course, Kyle doesn't remember the assignment, so he doesn't bring his math book home. Then, even if he remembers what he's supposed to do, he doesn't have the needed materials to get it done. Unfortunately for him, the teacher is going to expand on the discussion of order of operations tomorrow, taking for granted that what she talked about previously was reinforced by the homework.

When Kyle doesn't complete the assignment, he not only gets a zero for failing to turn it in, but he also won't understand everything the teacher is talking about the next day. He remembers that multiplication comes before addition, but once she adds exponents into the mix, he gets confused because he didn't get the extra practice everyone else did. And before he knows it, he is getting a bad grade in math, a subject in which he has no underlying academic weakness.

Lots of kids naturally become more organized as they mature, but kids like Kyle do not. Without external systems to help them, their desks, lockers, backpacks, and rooms quickly descend into chaos.

Think of it like learning to swim. Some kids jump right in the pool and figure it out on their own. Others require months or even years of patient, deliberate instruction just to learn to survive in the water, let alone swim laps or races. Any kids who are not naturally organized will need patient, consistent support to help them learn to do what may come completely naturally to others.

In addition to the struggles caused by executive function weaknesses, our lives are much more complicated than they used to be. According to the *Boston Globe*, the average American home has over 300,000 items![21] Kids are constantly outgrowing clothes, changing sports and activities, and collecting new toys and books.

> Any kids who are not naturally organized will need patient, consistent support to help them learn to do what may come completely naturally to others.

And as we've already mentioned, kids are bombarded by digital distractions that would have been unimaginable just a generation ago. Between gaming consoles and multiple social media platforms, we parents are tasked with helping our children navigate a world we hardly understand ourselves. So if you feel like your home is drowning in clutter—real and electronic—you're not alone!

But the good news is that you *don't* have to become a hardcore minimalist or banish electronics from your home to help your kids keep their schoolwork organized. Before we get into the techniques themselves, let's quickly break down the process of homework completion, so it will be clear how each technique supports each step.

UNDERSTANDING THE PROCESS OF HOMEWORK COMPLETION

Successfully completing and turning in homework is actually a complicated, multi-step process. For well-organized students and adults, most of these steps come naturally. But for students who tend towards disorganization, each is a potential trap for misplacing items and forgetting deadlines. We'll talk about steps 1, 2, and 5 in depth in this chapter. We'll tackle steps 3 and 4 (which relate to helping our kids organize their time) in Chapter 4.

1. **Students must accurately record their assignments with enough detail to complete them correctly.**

   When my own son entered middle school, it felt like a part time job just to help him keep track of his homework. Often, he didn't write everything down, because he figured he could just check his online homework portal later that night. But we soon discovered that not every teacher posted regularly on the homework portal. And the ones who did didn't always post in same way.

   Between the multiple folders on Blackboard.com and Google Docs, it could take us 20 minutes just to figure out what was due for one class!

   So kids really need to learn to write down their assignments in class when the teacher is explaining them. For students like Kyle, this really can be one of the most difficult parts of the process. After all, once class is over, students are understandably eager to get out of that desk, spend a couple of minutes socializing, and get to their next class.

In a perfect world, all our kids would learn to write down their teachers' instructions in an assignment book. And we should encourage this behavior as much as possible, because the physical act of writing actually helps the brain internalize the information better.[22]

Writing things down is most realistic when the teacher has the assignment written on the board at the beginning of class. Students are relatively alert, and they can record information quickly and accurately.

But often the teacher gives out the homework (or flashes the assignment on the promethium board) at the end of class. In these cases, older children with phones may find it easier to take a picture of the assignment on the board or screen. This requires very little effort, but it gets them in the habit of using the online portal as a backup instead of relying on it regularly.

2. Students must bring the necessary materials home

Few things are as aggravating as a student who has to read a passage and answer questions for science class but leaves his science book at school. Most of the time, the best solution is to have your kids get into the habit of bringing every book home every day. This way, they never have to worry about not having what they need.

Some schools have addressed this problem by having a classroom set of books to be used at school and allowing kids to keep their issued copies of the textbooks at home. In this case, you just need to figure out the best place to store the textbooks when they're not in use. This could be in the child's room, or you may want to dedicate a shelf or two in the living room or home office to storing school books.

When younger children are sitting down to start their homework, it can be helpful to lay out the materials they need for them. This way, they don't have to waste valuable mental energy trying to find things once they get going. Older kids can be encouraged to do this for themselves before they start.

3. **Students must set aside sufficient time to complete the assignment to an acceptable standard**
Disorganized students often have great difficulty assessing how much time an assignment will take to complete to an acceptable standard. Kids like Kyle are notorious for over-estimating how much time they have and underestimating how long each assignment will take. In the next chapter, we'll talk a lot more about strategies to help your child learn to be more realistic in their time assessments.

4. **Students must stay focused and complete the assignment in the allotted time**
Obviously, this is where children who have ADHD or executive function weaknesses will struggle the most. We'll cover ways to help them avoid distractions and finish their work as efficiently as possible in the next chapter.

5. **Students must remember to bring the completed work back to school and turn it in**

This is one area where online portals have really helped, as some teachers now allow students to turn in assignments electronically from home. Even teachers who generally collect papers may be willing to accommodate an ADHD or scattered child who finds it easier to email her homework to the teacher as soon as it's complete.

But using the computer doesn't automatically solve all organizational problems. After all, how many of us have saved a document or downloaded a file, only to struggle to find it later? Help your kids set up a sensible electronic filing system (either on the computer or within Google Drive) for their schoolwork or engage the help of a tutor. A single folder for schoolwork, with subfolders for each class, is an easy place to start. (We'll cover strategies for organizing physical papers in the next section.)

Identifying which of these steps gives your child the most trouble is a very important part of offering him or her the right support to get organized. Of course, many kids with executive function weaknesses struggle with all five steps. That's okay. Helping them get and stay organized will still go a long way toward relieving stress and enabling them to focus on other problem areas.

THE ORGANIZATIONAL ARSENAL: PRACTICAL TOOLS TO STAY ON TRACK

Every family with a Kyle will find success organizing their possessions in different ways, depending on factors such as the ages and number of their children and the amount of space available in the home. There is no "right" or "wrong" way to get organized. It's just whatever works best for your family.

That said, there are many practical strategies you can try to help your children with executive function weaknesses get organized and develop healthy, helpful habits to stay organized. Don't feel as though you have to try all of these at once. In fact, it may be easier to tackle them one at a time.

Consider starting with something you feel most confident about and sticking with it until it becomes relatively automated for your family. Then you can build on that success.

BASIC STRATEGIES

Basic strategies can be implemented in a straightforward way, without any outside help. These are little steps that can make a big difference!

The Launching Pad

What is it? A container that holds everything a child needs to take to school

What problem does it solve? Lost homework and chaotic mornings

How to get started: Find a bin or basket large enough to hold your child's backpack and any other materials needed for school and set up a time to talk to your child about the new strategy

"I can't find my worksheet!"

"Mom, you have to sign my permission slip for the field trip, or I can't go!"

"Who took my lacrosse stick? I put it right here!"

As we've already discussed, mornings can be crazy. Everyone is rushing around, trying to get ready for school and work and to leave the house on time. Add a disorganized child into the mix, and it's a recipe for chaos and stress.

The Launching Pad won't make the bus wait, but it *will* save everyone a lot of headaches in the morning. The Launching Pad is just any kind of bin that is large enough the hold your child's backpack and anything else he or she needs to bring to school. It gets filled each night, so that everything is ready in the morning.

Once you've deployed this tool, kids aren't "done" with their homework until their work is in their backpack, and their backpack is in the Launching Pad. The same goes for sports equipment and anything else they need for the next day. This frees kids up to use mornings to focus on getting dressed, eating breakfast and brushing teeth, and frees you up from having to worry if they're forgetting anything.

The Homework Caddy

What is it? A container that holds all the materials needed to complete homework assignments

What problem does it solve? Time wasted looking for pencils, paper, calculator, etc.

How to get started: Find an appropriate container and determine where to store it when not in use

Some materials for homework go back and forth to school, but some stay at home. When children struggle with procrastination, you don't want them wasting time looking for pencils and pens before they get started. You want their supplies in one place, but, as we discussed in the last chapter, you also want them to be able to work productively in many different locations.

A perfect solution is the Homework Caddy: a container that holds homework supplies like paper, post-it notes, pens, pencils, highlighters, and a scientific calculator for older kids. The Homework Caddy can be moved from the dining room table to the living room floor or even to the local library. It's another simple way to make life easier and homework completion smoother.

The Clean Sweep

What is it? A weekly 20-minute period when everyone in the house gets organized

What problem does it solve? The buildup of clutter in backpacks and study areas

How to get started: Set up a time to talk to your children about the new strategy and then set a recurring appointment on your phone (and have older children do the same)

Unimportant papers make it really hard to find important ones.

Even when children manage to hang onto worksheets and study guides, they may have trouble locating them when they need them. This is usually because their backpacks and desks are cluttered with everything they've collected since the beginning of the school year.

This is where the Clean Sweep can be a real life-saver.

The Clean Sweep is a weekly period of about 20 minutes when everyone in the family clears out some clutter and gets organized. Students go through their desks and backpacks, sort through their papers, organize electronic files on their computers and drives, and tidy up their study areas. Parents can get in on the action by cleaning out a junk drawer or going through briefcases and purses.

The Clean Sweep helps kids start each week fresh and organized. I encourage parents to set a recurring appointment in their phones and have older kids do the same. Everything won't be quite as pristine as it was at the beginning of the school year, but it will be a vast improvement.

As we discussed in the last chapter, one of the easiest ways to encourage a new habit is to tie it to an old one. For example, if you always eat a family meal on Sundays, you could do the Clean Sweep right before or right after Sunday dinner. It's also something that could be done before or after a sports activity or a football game that you watch as a family. When everyone knows it's coming and works together, the Clean Sweep really doesn't feel like much of a burden. And best of all, you get to enjoy the benefits all week!

Remember to look for effort, not perfect results. It takes disorganized children a while to learn to manage these kinds of activities on their own, so do praise them for trying. If they try consistently, they *will* improve. And eventually, like all the habits we discussed in the last chapter, the Clean Sweep can go on autopilot.

ADVANCED STRATEGIES

Advanced organizational strategies involve more adjustment and effort from the disorganized. These can also be introduced by the parent, but many times, kids will be more receptive to another adult. A tutor or organizational coach can sometimes feel like a more neutral party, since parents typically offer feedback and advice on every aspect of a child's life.

Monthly/Quarterly Archiving and Backpack Clean up

What is it? A monthly or quarterly appointment to go through every folder and binder

What problem does it solve? The buildup of outdated papers

How to get started: Set a reminder and have your children go through all school folders and binders on their own or with a tutor

Once a month or quarter, you can extend the Clean Sweep for a more thorough organizing session. Children can empty their backpacks entirely and put loose papers into three piles. I use the acronym KAT for the Keep pile, the Archive pile and the Toss pile. The Keep pile gets filed back into correct subject folders or binders, while the Toss pile gets thrown away. The Archive pile can be clipped together and stored in a bin or a Pendaflex folder. If kids need to go back and locate something later, they will know that the more recent papers are toward the top.

Children can then repeat the KAT sorting process with each individual binder and folder, throwing out papers that are no longer needed, but archiving old tests, quizzes and study guides that they'll need for cumulative exams.

These days, backpacks seem to be taking the place of lockers in many schools, so they fill up very quickly. Kids can become protective and defensive about the contents of their backpacks and may resist their parents' attempts to help them deal with the clutter. In these cases, it may be helpful to have a tutor or organizational coach help your child go through the backpack and teach them how to sort through their papers. Then you can support them as they repeat the process at home.

The Homework Folder

What is it? A single folder to hold all homework assignments

What problem does it solve? Assignments that get lost on the way home or never make it into the teacher's hands

How to get started: Purchase a sturdy two-pocket folder and label the left pocket "To do" and the right pocket "Done"

Kids like Kyle have no system for where they put important papers. Sometimes they put them in a folder, while other times they stick them in a book, into their pockets, or stuff them down in the bottom of the backpack. This makes it very difficult to find their assignments when it's time to get them done *and* when it's time to turn them in.

A study conducted at Penn State[23] on children like Kyle who were underperforming because of disorganization found that having disorganized students use a Homework Folder was the most helpful intervention for improving grades.

Usually, kids will have a separate folder, binder or section of a binder for each academic subject. The Homework Folder is simply a durable two-pocket folder that kids keep with them for *all* their classes. When they receive an assignment from a teacher *in any class*, they place it in the left hand "To Do" pocket of the Homework Folder. When they finish an assignment at home, they place it in the right hand "Done" pocket of the Homework Folder.

This simple system can be very helpful for kids who struggle with steps 2 and 5 of the homework process: bringing the needed materials home and ensuring that the completed assignment makes it back to school and into the teacher's hands.

The To Do pocket of the Homework Folder also helps children create a list of assignments when they begin their homework. They should keep some blank sheets of paper in the To Do pocket, so that any assignments that are written on the board or given online can be written on the paper. This helps children remember work that doesn't come with a physical handout.

If an assignment is completed online, the paper that had that assignment can be transferred to the Done folder or thrown away. The work in the Done folder is then handed in to the teacher. If the teacher checks it off for completion and then gives the paper back, it should then be filed in the binder.

The Homework Folder is a relatively simple intervention, but it does involve a lot of buy-in from students. They have to change the way they handle assignments all day long. Because of this, it can be helpful to have a tutor explain the process and get them on board.

When high schooler Alexis came to our tutoring center, her backpack, folders, and binders were a mess. She rarely had any idea what her assignments were, and when she did do her homework, she often failed to turn it in. As you might imagine, there were a lot of zeros on her homework portal, and they were dragging down her grades.

After a few meetings with one of our tutors, Alexis began using a homework folder. With the help of her parents, she began performing a weekly Clean Sweep of her backpack and desk. Not only did she begin completing and turning in her assignments more consistently, she made the fourth quarter honor roll and sustained her success the following year!

Binder Clips for Block Scheduling

What is it? Two sets of binder clips to label folders, binders, and text books

What problem does it solve? Uncertainty about which materials to bring to school on which days

How to get started: Purchase binder clips in two different colors

A growing number of schools have moved to block scheduling. This means students attend only half their classes on a given day, but for twice the length of time. There are many great educational reasons for this choice, which gives instructors more flexibility to offer longer lessons, labs, and activities. But for kids with executive function weaknesses, the change in routine from day to day can present an extra challenge to overcome.

One practical way to help kids remember which materials they need to bring to school on which days is to use binder clips of two different colors, one for the "A" day and one for the "B" day. (Some schools have block schedules identified by odd and even, or even two colors, often the school colors. In this latter case, you might try to purchase binder clips in the appropriate colors to match the color for that day.)

For example, if you choose red and blue, you would put red clips on all the folders, binders and textbooks needed for A days, and blue clips on all the materials needed for the B days. For any materials they need for both A and B days, simply place both clips on the binder, book or folder. This enables children to quickly figure out which materials they need for each day.

TURN IN YOUR BADGE

Kyle's parents set up a time to talk to him about implementing the Launching Pad strategy after dinner. Instead of lecturing him on the importance of being organized and responsible, as they had in the past, they tried a different approach.

"So, we've noticed that you often get your homework done, but you sometimes have trouble finding it when it's time to turn it in to the teacher," his dad began.

"That's not true!" Kyle protested. "I remembered to turn it in yesterday!"

"Kyle," his mother said gently, "we're not angry. We just want to work together to make sure you get credit for the work you do. We're going to try setting up a Launching Pad. It's a bin we put by the door to hold your backpack and your soccer cleats. That way everything will be ready for you when you leave to catch the bus. Does that sound okay?"

Kyle nodded, and his parents explained that from now on, his homework was only done when everything was in the backpack and the backpack was in the Launching Pad. Kyle squirmed a bit but agreed to try the new system.

With help from his parents, Kyle set an alert on his phone so that every night at 9:30, it reminded him to put his materials in his backpack and his backpack in the Launching Pad. His parents were careful to express their appreciation for his efforts, and his dad even got him a new comic book at the end of two weeks to reward him.

The most immediate result of these new systems was a reduction in morning stress. Kyle's parents used to feel like they had to inspect his backpack and interrogate him about whether he had everything. Now they felt reasonably confident that he was leaving for school with what he needed.

I'd love to tell you that from this point on, Kyle never misplaced an assignment again. But as you might imagine, one afternoon, his mother checked his grades and saw that dreaded zero for a science worksheet. She set up a time to talk with him about it after soccer practice.

She explained that she had noticed the missing assignment. Then, instead of asking him *why* he had forgotten to turn it in, she asked, "*Going forward*, what do you think you can do to make sure you don't miss another assignment?"

This simple change in a few words kept Kyle from feeling defensive and got him thinking about his own actions and decisions. He agreed to meet with a tutor, who showed him how to use a Homework Folder to keep track of his assignments.

This was one more step in Kyle's journey to get organized and take responsibility for his schoolwork. Instead of telling him what to do, his mother encouraged him to think through the options before him and make the right choice for himself.

This simple change in a few words kept Kyle from feeling defensive and got him thinking about his own actions and decisions.

Kyle didn't become a perfect student overnight. But he did improve a great deal and became enthusiastic about school again. And, most importantly, he got more of the tools he needed for long-term success.

A QUICK RECAP

- Disorganization can negatively affect every area of life. It causes smart kids to fall behind in multiple subjects and creates stress for everyone.

- Some kids will never become organized without outside support systems and patient instruction. You do not need to have a perfectly organized home to offer helpful support.

- Homework completion is a complicated, multi-step process. Kids with executive function weaknesses may need external support for any and all steps.

- There are both basic and advanced strategies you can implement to support your child's organizational development. Any family can implement the basic ones on its own; a tutor or coach may be helpful for implementing advanced strategies.

- Use proactive communication and powerful questions to talk with your children about organization. Praise and encourage effort and improvement.

4

Mastering Time Struggles

"How's that paper going?" Julie's dad asks with a raised eyebrow.

"Okay," she sighs, hoping she can somehow "will" it to completion

In reality, the paper is not going at all. Julie is a good kid, and she wants to make her parents happy. But the more her dad asks her about the paper, the more stressed out she gets.

Julie got the assignment two weeks ago, and she really has been trying to work on it. She has spent hours looking at the handout with the grading rubric and trying to think of what to say. She's also tried to research some ideas on the internet, but too often she ends up on Pinterest, thinking about ideas for redecorating her room.

Every now and then, Julie will type a sentence or two. But then she'll get stuck again. Now the due date is two days away, and she only has three paragraphs written. And her dad—who has never missed a deadline in his life—is beside himself with frustration.

"SUPER BOWL" KIDS AND THE TIME MANAGEMENT STRUGGLE

Kids like Julie are what I call "Super Bowl" kids. Each February, the Super Bowl takes up at least four hours on TV, but only one of those hours involves actual football. The rest of the time is taken up by timeouts, a lengthy halftime show, and endless commercials. This ratio of productivity to fluff is fine for an entertaining sport, but not so great when it comes to schoolwork!

Super Bowl kids can spend hours each day in front of their homework, but they end up having very little to show for it. This frustrates their parents, of course, but it also frustrates them. They feel as though they are trying their best, but they just aren't getting the results they want, because their executive function weaknesses make it difficult to focus.

Students with weak executive function almost always struggle with managing their time. They often have trouble getting started with their work, which can have a couple of underlying causes. Kids like Julie tend to be anxious about school, whereas bright but disorganized kids like Kyle just can't muster the motivation to get going.

Many of these kids are also easily distracted once they do get going, because they have trouble directing their attention

Students with weak executive function almost always struggle with managing their time.

to the task at hand. This can turn a simple worksheet into long, drawn-out torture for everyone involved. Since not all time struggles are exactly the same, accurately diagnosing the problem can help us select the most effective intervention to try.

TIME STRUGGLE #1:
THE "SOFT" INTERNAL CLOCK PROBLEM

Students like Julie and Kyle also have a hard time determining how long different assignments will take. This is actually a very common problem for many of us. Adults and children alike regularly underestimate how long we will need to complete a task.[24] Just think about how many grownup projects go past their original deadlines, whether it is a home renovation or bringing a new product to market!

> Because kids regularly overestimate how quickly they will be able to finish something, they do not allot enough time in their schedule to complete it.

Because kids regularly overestimate how quickly they will be able to finish something, they do not allot enough time in their schedule to complete it. Conversely, they may also dread an assignment—because they think it will take forever—when it really won't take that long once they get going.

My friend and colleague, Dr. Ari Tuckman, explains our perception of the passage of time in terms of an "internal clock" we all possess. For some of us, the clock ticks loudly, making us very aware of how much time is passing while we are going about our daily lives and activities. For others, like Julie and Kyle, it ticks softly. They just aren't naturally aware of how much time is going by, whether they're watching a movie or trying to get homework done.

People like Julie's dad are lucky enough to have loud internal clocks. He almost always shows up to work early and is much better than most people at judging how long a task is going to take. This means he allows ample time to complete a project, cook dinner, or get to the airport. Not surprisingly, he is also great at planning ahead. He anticipates the possibility of obstacles like traffic and makes allowances for them. He loves the feeling of being on top of things and ahead of the game.

Julie's dad never really had to learn any of these skills, because they just came naturally to him. Because of this, he gets easily frustrated with his daughter and has no idea how to help her.

The important thing to remember is that these differences come from the way our brains function. They are not a result of a parenting mistake or a bad teacher. Fortunately, there are simple steps we can take to help kids with soft internal clocks pay attention to the passage of time, compensate for their weaknesses, and improve their ability to plan ahead.

TIME STRUGGLE #2:
THE TIME HORIZON PROBLEM

Julie's paper might seem like a straightforward assignment, but like so many things in life, it is a complicated, multi-step process that she doesn't naturally understand how to manage. First, she needs to develop a thesis statement. Then, according to the rubric, she should find three sources, take notes on them, and write an outline. After that, she should write approximately twelve paragraphs of content, including an introduction and a conclusion. Finally, she needs to create a bibliography listing her sources. (And all that is just for the first draft!)

Long-term assignments like this compound a child's struggles with time management. Science projects, research papers, and studying for cumulative exams require planning over several days or even weeks. This means breaking down the task into individual steps, estimating how long each step will take, and finding time in an already overcrowded schedule.

For kids like Julie, all that feels very overwhelming.

Great planners often have loud internal clocks *and* long time horizons. A time horizon can be thought of as a period of time covered by a plan. Corporations or investors think about planning over a quarterly, yearly, or even decade-long time horizon. In our personal lives, we may plan for goals over periods of weeks, months, or years.

Kids with longer time horizons are able to think about a test at the end of the week and mentally divide up the necessary studying. They can figure out on their own that they should review important concepts on Tuesday, since they have a play rehearsal on Wednesday. They know that by Thursday, they want to be reviewing information they are already familiar with, instead of trying to cram new ideas into their heads at the last minute.

As you might expect, kids with soft internal clocks typically have shorter time horizons as well. They struggle to plan more than a day—or even an hour—ahead. Just as they don't really notice the minutes and hours passing by, a test that's three days away may seem as far in the future as six months from now. This means that deadlines just don't feel real to them until they get really, really close.

Kids with soft internal clocks typically have shorter time horizons as well. They struggle to plan more than a day–or even an hour–ahead.

Often this habit is so ingrained that kids with short time horizons honestly believe waiting until the last minute is the only way to get things done. For kids like these, it's important to help them lengthen their time horizons and patiently teach them to plan ahead, which we'll address later on in this chapter.

Watch out for Functional Procrastinators!

Kids with short time horizons may be either functional or dysfunctional procrastinators. Functional procrastinators will usually get their work done and maintain acceptable grades, even though they don't get started until the last minute.

Dysfunctional procrastinators will often panic, leading to missing assignments and poor grades.

At first glance, it might seem like the dysfunctional procrastinators have the bigger problem. After all, they are the ones suffering the consequences of their procrastination. But functional procrastinators—especially those who perform well in high school without planning ahead—may be unknowingly setting themselves up for even greater problems later.

The inability to plan ahead *will* catch up with these kids eventually, even if it's not until they are faced with more challenging college work or their first job. (For more on this, see the bonus chapter, The College Procrastinator.) That's why it's so important to get functional procrastinators to lengthen their time horizons, even if their current grades are acceptable. Teaching kids the habit of thinking ahead will help them prepare for these future responsibilities.

TIME STRUGGLE #3:
THE STALLED ENGINE PROBLEM

Did you ever have a car that just wouldn't start? You'd turn the key and—although the engine would rev and turn over—for some reason it just couldn't get going. That's how some kids are with their homework. Like Julie, they sit in front of a book or laptop, fidgeting or daydreaming. Meanwhile, precious minutes are slipping by, and nothing is getting done.

As I've mentioned, some kids struggle to get started because of apathy while others deal with anxiety. Apathetic kids just can't seem to motivate themselves to get going, while anxious kids feel paralyzed by fear. In both cases, we want to help them start their homework by making it feel less demanding and intimidating.

Just as that stalled car runs fine when the engine finally gets going, once kids are working, it's much easier for them to continue until everything is done. In Chapter 2, I talked about establishing routines for the time and place for homework. Later in this chapter, we'll look at routines that help students actually get to work.

Just as that stalled car runs fine when the engine finally gets going, once kids are working, it's much easier for them to continue until everything is done.

GETTING THE INTERNAL CLOCK TO TICK LOUDER

There are several simple interventions that can help your child's soft internal clock tick a little louder. These are not magic bullets that will instantly solve the problem, but rather, tools that will help them gradually improve.

Make Use of Analog Clocks, Watches, and Special Timers

Digital clocks are great, but they don't do quite as good a job at showing us the passage of time as an analog clock. Analog clocks give us a visual representation of the seconds, minutes, and hours going by as the hands make their trip around the clock face. This can be very valuable for kids with soft internal clocks.

Placing large-faced analog clocks in your children's rooms and other areas where they study is a very easy way to help them become more aware of how much time is passing while they are playing or doing homework. The same goes for an analog watch that they can wear and look at throughout the day.

There are also special digital timers that display a circle representing the amount of time that the timer has been set for. As the seconds and minutes tick by, the corresponding percentage of the circle disappears, once again giving a visual sense of the passage of time. These timers may be very helpful, especially for younger children.

Create a Distraction-Free Environment

We want our kids' study areas to be as distraction-free as reasonably possible. At a minimum, this means keeping the television off and having people take their conversations to another part of the house. But what about the child's phone?

Adults and children alike are distracted by their phones. Between text messages, notifications, and social media alerts, it's amazing any of us get anything done! But taking a phone away from a child often feels like a punishment, and most parents are hesitant to do this except under extreme circumstances.

A great strategy to help your kids study without actually taking away their phones is to have them place their phones in a location where they would have to physically get up from their seats to retrieve them. This enables children to be in the same room with their phones but removes a lot of the device's distracting power. Every twenty minutes or so, the children can get up and check their phones for a minute or two, and then return to their work.

Use Apps to Stay on Task

Computers are wonderful tools for productivity, but they can also be endless sources of distraction. How many times have you been working on a project, only to find yourself surfing the internet for something completely unrelated?

But with more and more schoolwork being done and turned in on computers, digital distractions are definitely here to stay. So how do you help your children stay focused when they must be on their computers to do research, write papers, and turn in work?

Thankfully, some great software developers have created apps to help with these problems. Here are a few that students in my tutoring center have used with great success:

Self-control (for Mac) and *Stay Focused* (for PC) enable users to block distracting websites for a set period of time. For example, children can choose to block Netflix, YouTube, Pinterest or various social media sites for 20 minutes. During that 20 minutes, even restarting the computer or closing the app will not allow them to access these sources of distraction. Often just making the decision to block these sites helps students focus.

Rescue Time runs in the background of a phone or computer, tracking the time spent on various applications and websites. It then generates a report that shows you how you (or your child) actually spent the day. You can even set alerts to let you know when you've spent a certain amount of time on a particular activity. This is a great option for older children who don't realize how much time they are spending watching You-Tube videos or checking Twitter.

Forest is another great app to help kids stay away from their smartphones or tablets while they study. The app causes a digital tree to grow on the home screen during a period of time that you set. If you try to use your device during that time, the poor tree withers and dies. Each time you stay off your phone for the chosen amount of time, you can add a new tree to your forest.

The best part about these apps, and others like them, is that they put the children in control of potential distractions and enable them to take ownership of their time. These are invaluable skills as they grow up and take on more responsibilities.

LENGTHENING TIME HORIZONS

Our time horizons lengthen as we mature, but sometimes they need a little help. Here are a couple strategies to encourage growing kids to start thinking ahead.

Make Your Weekends Count

One of the best ways to help your children lengthen their time horizons is to make the most of the weekend. Between busy work schedules, extracurricular activities, and school, most of us end up with very little down time between Monday and Friday. And of course, many kids (understandably!) don't want to think about school over the weekend. This means that kids with short time horizons show up to school each Monday with little to no clue about what's going to happen over the next few days. Taking the time over the weekend to talk about the week ahead can really help kids lengthen their time horizons. Looking at a physical or electronic calendar and writing down their appointments and deadlines helps them begin to visualize longer periods of time and think ahead. These skills will not develop overnight, of course, but with consistent attention they will noticeably improve.

The Clean Sweep Extension

Once you've established the Clean Sweep routine, you can consider extending it to include a discussion of the week ahead. (As we've already mentioned, attaching a new routine to an existing one makes it easier to put on autopilot!) The meeting doesn't need to be long, but it should cover important school assignments, as well as extracurricular activities and family events. In addition to writing things down on a physical calendar, you may want to have older children enter alerts and appointments into an electronic calendar on their phones and laptops.

A really great strategy is to begin the meeting with some of the child's favorite activities and build the rest of the schedule around those. For example, if your son is going to a sleepover on Saturday night, you could write that down first. Then you could work backwards, asking, "What do you need to get done *before* the sleepover to make sure you don't have to worry about schoolwork while you're there?"

This is also a great opportunity to help them think through how to utilize those "weird windows of time" between activities.

Your child can set an alert to study French vocabulary on the bus ride home from school or research a paper topic at the school library between the time school ends and basketball practice starts. This not only lightens the burden of homework when kids get home, but it also enables them to practice planning ahead.

We can also support the development of shorter term planning skills to help kids get the most out of each study session. One way to do this is to have them create a concrete, prioritized task list each day. For younger children, this may mean actually writing out a list, or laying out their materials in front them. Older children can copy a list you create and eventually learn to create their own.

The list can be written in an assignment book, on a white board or even just on a post-it note. For kids who are extremely resistant to writing things down by hand, the list can be entered into their phones or on a computer.

JUMP STARTING THE ENGINE

There are several simple ways to help kids get going on their work, and not every way will work with every kid. Experiment and see which one is best for your child.

A Little Time

One strategy to get kids started on homework is to set a timer for a short amount time—between 5 and 15 minutes—and have children commit to work as hard as they can until the timer stops. For younger kids my tutors and I sometimes call this "Five Minutes of Fury," because *anyone* can work furiously for five minutes. For older kids, it's the "Tolerable Ten," for the same reason: most of us can tolerate just about anything for only ten minutes. When the timer is finished, they can either take a quick break or keep going.

You may also want to consider setting the timer for "odd" times like 7 or 13 minutes. Numbers that end in five or zero make arithmetic easier, but unusual times help us think a little more precisely. (This is why I schedule one of my weekly staff meetings for 8:42 AM. People are much less likely to be late!)

A lot of apathetic kids have a vague feeling that their homework is going to take forever, so they might as well put it off as long as possible. Committing to work for a short period of time eliminates that dread. Remember, you're not roping them into finishing an assignment right away. You're just helping start that engine!

A Little Task

Kids who are feeling anxious about their schoolwork may find more success getting started with a small task. For example, a student could commit to writing out the definition of five vocabulary words or doing three math problems. This works great for worksheets that are naturally divided into problems or exercises, but it may require support from a parent or tutor for larger assignments such as essays.

For longer term projects, your children may need you to work with them to break down the steps needed to complete it. For example, Julie's father eventually helped her create a task list for her paper that included forming a thesis statement, doing research, creating an outline, and so on. Similarly, a science project could be broken down into the steps of selecting a topic, doing preliminary research, developing a hypothesis, developing an experiment to test the hypothesis, performing the experiment, and reviewing the data. Then the student could begin writing the paper and putting together the display board.

When you break the assignment down into smaller units, kids can see that a huge project is really just a series of manageable tasks. Then you can help them place all these tasks onto a calendar, so that your children can immediately see if they are hitting the right benchmarks to complete it on time.

Instead of just asking her how things were going, Julie's father eventually learned to encourage her to start with a clearly defined, manageable task, like writing an outline and or writing topic sentences for each of her paragraphs. Then she could take a break, check her phone, or keep going. In Julie's case, once she got going, she was more motivated to continue. She could finally feel herself making progress and could see on her task list and calendar how that progress would take her to her goal.

These short spurts of work and concentration are much more productive for kids who find the thought of tackling all their homework at once unappealing or intimidating. Instead of being annoyed by constant reminders, they are encouraged by making progress. And it's this feeling of encouragement that fuels them to the finish line.

Other Applications of Time and Task

Many kids who have trouble getting started on homework also struggle with cleaning their rooms or taking care of other responsibilities around the house. You can use the same time or task technique to help get them going. For example, you can set a timer and have them clean up as much as they can for five or ten minutes, or you could ask them to put away all their toys or straighten up all their clothes before taking a break.

Another helpful technique is to take a picture of the clean room and display it for the child to see. This gives them a visual representation of what they are trying to accomplish. It also reminds them that they have done this before, and they can do it again!

TURN IN YOUR BADGE

When Julie's father first tried to help her with her planning skills, he took his natural understanding of the passage of time for granted. He didn't realize how difficult this skill was for his daughter to learn. This led to tremendous frustration for both of them.

Once he understood that he had a loud internal clock, while Julie had a soft one, he became more patient with her. In addition to helping her lengthen her time horizons, he learned to stop nagging her about planning and try productive solutions instead.

As with other strategies, visual and electronic reminders really help us turn in our badges and stop being the homework police. When communicating with our kids about time management, powerful questions that prompt them to think are far more effective than just telling them what to do. Remember, children tend to become defensive when they are procrastinating, so questions should be open-ended and non-judgmental.

When communicating with our kids about time management, powerful questions that prompt them to think are far more effective than just telling them what to do.

Instead of telling Julie to work on her paper, Julie's father began asking, "What's the most important thing you can get done right now that will help you make progress?" This got Julie thinking about the project as a whole and how to prioritize her tasks.

Instead of directly telling apathetic procrastinators that they are being unrealistic about how long something will take, try asking, "How long did it take you the last time you tried an assignment like this?" Again, this gets them thinking for themselves.

Lastly, if you have tried these strategies and feel like you are not making enough progress, it may be time to enlist the help of a coach or tutor. Sometimes kids just need to talk to another trusted adult about their struggles before they are willing to try something new.

A QUICK RECAP

- Kids with executive function weaknesses often struggle to manage their time effectively.

- Kids (and adults!) naturally resist starting tasks they perceive as unpleasant.

- Children with soft internal clocks simply don't notice how much time is passing when they are doing something enjoyable. They may also underestimate how long an assignment will take. Try analog clocks and distraction-fighting apps to help the clock tick louder.

- Students with short time horizons struggle to plan ahead. A project due in three days might as well be due in a month. Try setting an appointment to discuss the week ahead and utilizing a planning calendar to help lengthen time horizons.

- When kids struggle to get started, having them work for a short amount of time or on a short task can be an effective way to get them going.

- Rather than just telling them what to do, utilize powerful questions to communicate with your children about time struggles.

5

Mastering Subject Struggles

The year was 1983. Michael Jackson and The Police were topping the charts, *Flashdance* and *Return of the Jedi* were packing crowds into the theaters, and *Three's Company* had everyone in tears of laughter in front of the TV. I was in eighth grade and loving everything about it.

Everything except algebra.

It wasn't that I hated math. In fact, I sat right in the front of the class, doing my best to follow everything the teacher said. Yet the more he droned on, the more my mind wandered. I could feel my muscles tensing up, starting in my back, traveling through my shoulders to my neck. Sometimes my head was throbbing by the end of class.

Each day that went by, algebra made less sense, and I got further behind. By the fourth week of school, I had no idea how to do my homework. I would just write down random numbers under the problems, so I could get credit for trying. I began to feel like a failure, which sapped my enthusiasm for school. Even subjects I used to love—like English and social studies—became a drag.

Thankfully, my parents noticed what was going on and decided to intervene.

My dad was an engineer, so he seemed like the natural person to help. I still remember sitting with him at my little Ethan Allen desk, poring over variables and linear equations. But by the end of the study session, my soft-spoken father was so frustrated that he threw my math book across the room!

First, I couldn't understand what my teacher was talking about, and now I couldn't understand my own dad. What was wrong with me?

DIAGNOSING THE SOURCE OF THE STRUGGLE

Sometimes our kids' struggles with procrastination go beyond issues with time management. Their reluctance to get to work may reflect a genuine academic difficulty with the content itself. I wasn't procrastinating on my math homework because I was undisciplined or apathetic; I simply didn't know how to do the problems.

But *why* didn't I know how to do the problems? I was going to class, sitting in the front, doing my absolute best to pay attention. My math performance in previous years indicated that I was ready for algebra. What was going on?

The first step toward helping kids with content struggles is to correctly identify the source of the problem.

"Swiss Cheese" Kids

Like many kids with executive function weaknesses, I was one of the Swiss Cheese Kids I mentioned in Chapter 1. I had holes in my knowledge of algebra, because I couldn't consistently

The first step toward helping kids with content struggles is to correctly identify the source of the problem.

focus on what the teacher was saying. In a cumulative subject like math, this meant I began to fall further and further behind.

Swiss Cheese Kids can excel in classes like literature or art where you don't necessarily have to pay extremely close attention every minute of class to know what's going on. They may also have success in one unit of a subject, only to struggle tremendously with another. Often, they themselves don't know why they are struggling and may feel just as confused and frustrated as their parents over their performance.

Thankfully, there are plenty of effective interventions for Swiss Cheese Kids, which we'll talk about in the next section. It's important to remember that the ability to pay attention for longer periods of time does improve with age, so our goal is often to help children keep up with their schoolwork until they are mature enough to do so on their own.

A Teaching Style Mismatch

Sometimes the teaching style in a particular class does not match a student's preferred learning style. In my case, my math teacher's style of lecturing uninterrupted for long periods of time really didn't work for me. I was more than capable of grasping the concepts, just not in the way he was presenting them.

Many educators have found it helpful to distinguish between three main styles of learning: visual, auditory, and kinesthetic.[25] Visual learners learn best from looking at pictures, maps, charts, graphs and other visual representations of data and ideas. Auditory learners learn easiest by listening to someone explain a concept. And kinesthetic learners grasp concepts more quickly when they use manipulatives and other tactile methods of learning.

Consider three children learning how to find the factors of the number 20. A visual learner might find it easiest to see the problem written out on a piece of paper or on a whiteboard. An auditory learner would probably prefer to have it explained orally, while a kinesthetic learner might grasp it best by taking 20 pennies and seeing how they can be divided up into two piles of ten, ten piles of two, four piles of five, and so on.

When the teaching style in a class doesn't match a student's preferred learning style, it can be easy to fall behind. That said, we actually learn best when we utilize all three modalities to study. (We'll talk a lot more about this in the next chapter.)

The "Negative Experience" Gap

A significantly negative experience in a subject can create long-term content struggles for some students. Teaching well is very hard work, and there are all sorts of challenges teachers face that are far beyond their control. But an ineffective or unkind teacher can have far-reaching effects on a student's performance in a particular subject for years to come.[26]

For example, suppose your child had terrific math teachers for first through third grade, but an ineffective teacher in fourth. Because of this teacher, your child never really learned how to add and subtract fractions reliably. But when he moves on to the next grade—although this concept will be reviewed—he may fall further behind because of what he didn't learn the previous year.

Kids can also experience emotional conflict with teachers. Of course, they probably aren't going to love every one of their instructors for every year of school. But if the experience with a teacher is unpleasant enough, it can actually cause them to be resistant to learning that subject in the future. Often kids don't realize this is going on. They just think they hate a certain subject or aren't good at it.

Similarly, students may become so frustrated with a single unit that they want to give up on the entire class. Maybe your daughter is taking chemistry and does great with molecular structure, calculating pH, and calorimetry. But when she gets to stoichiometry, she gets stuck. If this problem is not addressed promptly, it may sabotage her performance for the rest of the year.

A Class Too Far

Lastly, students will struggle with content if they are working at a developmentally inappropriate level. Many schools now push middle school students to take classes that were once reserved for high school, and early high school students to take college classes. Some sixth- and seventh-graders are being encouraged to take algebra, while ninth- and tenth-graders are placed in AP Physics or AP Biology. Anxious to put their kids in the best possible position to apply to college, parents go along.

Taking these classes so early may be the appropriate choice for a small minority of students, but for many bright kids, they will be unnecessarily taxing or even overwhelming. Remember, the specific age at which a student is ready for algebra or an AP class is not necessarily directly associated with their long-term potential for success in that subject. Some kids learn to walk at nine months old, others at fifteen months. But the nine-month walkers do not necessarily walk "better" in middle school than the fifteen-month walkers!

Of course, all students need to be in classes that challenge them sufficiently. But don't be afraid to move your children out of classes that are just too much for them right now. Taking honors history instead of AP government in tenth grade will not prevent them from getting into the college of their choice. It is much more important that they work at a level where they are both challenged and able to do the work proficiently, than that their transcripts show dozens of AP course starting in ninth grade.

GETTING UNSTUCK FROM SHORT-TERM STICKING POINTS

After reading through the four categories I just outlined, you may find that your child's "Swiss Cheese" isn't all that porous and he's just missing a few pieces of the puzzle. Maybe he just had a minor clash with a topic or a teacher and simply needs to spend some time revisiting that unit or assignment. Or maybe he's just encountered some difficult material that he's avoiding because he's not sure how to approach it. In these cases, a quick intervention from Mom or Dad may be just what the doctor ordered.

That said, when kids get stuck over how to complete a specific assignment in the ways I just mentioned, parents tend to respond in one of two way:

Response 1: *"You still can't figure it out? Move over and let me show you how to do it."*

Response 2: *"You know what? I already finished fifth grade, so this isn't my problem!"*

The first response will certainly get the job done, so it's understandable why so many parents choose it. Unfortunately, the more often we jump in and do the work for them, the fewer opportunities they have to figure things out on their own. In the long run, they need to learn to study effectively and independently. On the other hand, the second response may provide too little support, leading to a frustrated kid and an unhappy parent.

We want to strike that tricky balance between letting our kids feel supported while enabling them to grow and mature. There are several ways to do this. For many subjects, you can prompt your children to locate examples of similar questions or problems in their textbooks, study guides, or class notes. Looking at example problems will often help them figure out how to do the assignment. You can also help them set up the problem and let them work out the solution on their own.

There are also some great websites that can help students with content struggles. The **Khan Academy** has thousands of short instructional videos to help kids learn or practice specific kinds of problems in both math and science. They also have helpful videos for history, economics, and other subjects. Their website is easily searchable, so if your child simply needs a quick refresher on the stages of mitosis or how to multiply fractions, the Khan Academy is a great resource.

Crash Course is a YouTube channel that delivers highly entertaining television-style lessons on a variety of academic subjects. Each subject is broken down into bite-size episodes around ten minute each. So, if your student is facing a test on the Civil War or just struggling to make sense of a new philosophy class, Crash Course can come to the rescue. It's also great for reviewing and previewing in all the subjects they cover, which we'll discuss a little later on.

Rev is an online service that will create punctuated transcripts of audio recordings. This service can help children who have great difficulty writing papers, who are behind on a large assignment, or who just don't type quickly enough. (There is a fee for this service.)

WHEN THE SUBJECT STRUGGLE IS REAL

When a child's struggle with content goes beyond the short-term issues described above, it is important to intervene as soon as possible. If a student simply needs to move to a different class, the problem can usually be solved with a phone call or email to the guidance counselor. If you believe your child is in the correct class, but is simply struggling to keep up, then you must get her extra help as quickly as you can.

The First Challenge: Who Does The Helping?

The first option is to provide this extra help yourself. If you are comfortable with the content in question, you can try to offer extra support to your child. If she is a Swiss Cheese Kid, start by assessing where the gaps are in her knowledge and begin offering extra practice to fill them in. If there's a mismatch with the teaching style, try presenting the concepts in a way that makes better sense to her. And if she's had a negative experience with the subject in the past, try getting her to talk to you about how she's feeling.

It is very common for kids to push back against receiving help from their parents, so you will need to be prepared for resistance to your efforts. Don't be surprised if you hear, "That's not how Mrs. Jones says we're supposed to do it!" Kids, like all of us, don't like being told what to do, especially by their parents.

For example, if your elementary schooler seems to grasp the basic concepts, but is making careless mistakes, you may want to begin spot checking his work. Rather than going over every problem or exercise, select just a few items to check. Going over

For example, if your elementary schooler seems to grasp the basic concepts, but is making careless mistakes, you may want to begin spot checking his work.

these select items in detail can help him go back and fix any other mistakes, and it also gives you a good snapshot of his progress.

Of course, once our kids are in high school, there may be some content that we are not able to help with. After all, unless we are actively using calculus, it might be a little difficult to show our kids how to take a derivative or find the limit of a complicated equation. In these cases, it's probably best to enlist the help of a tutor. In the case of a Swiss Cheese Kid, this will not be a onetime event. If your child is behind, she will need consistent intervention until she is completely caught up. She may also need help to keep up for the rest of the semester or year.

Overlearning, Reviewing, and Previewing: How To Fill In The Holes

After my dad's attempt to tutor me didn't go so well, my mom stepped in and decided to hire a math tutor. I was outraged! I told my parents I understood math just fine, and the placement test I took at Beachside Learning Center proved I did. But after some arguing, I finally agreed to give it a try.

This turned out to make all the difference in the world. I needed someone to help me fill in the gaps in my understanding of algebra and help me master new concepts. But I also needed a subject matter expert who could present ideas in a way that made them easier for me to grasp, and that's just what my tutor, Mr. Rogo, did.

On top of that, Mr. Rogo showed me three new study techniques that transformed my education: *overlearning, reviewing, and previewing*. It turned out that I was one of those kids who simply needed more practice to master certain math skills. This didn't mean I *couldn't* learn algebra and learn it well. It also didn't mean that I wouldn't be able move on to master geometry, trigonometry, and calculus in the years ahead. I just had to have a little more repetition to be able to understand exactly what was going on and demonstrate that knowledge confidently and reliably on a test.

My tutor and I worked on each kind of problem so many times, it felt like we were "over-learning" them. But in reality, we were just practicing the skill over and over until it became second nature for me. It was like practicing a piece for a musical recital or rehearsing lines for a play. This not only helped me improve my test grades, but also gave me a greater sense of confidence moving forward and renewed my enthusiasm for school in general.

Mr. Rogo also taught me to regularly review concepts that I had already mastered. Rather than wait for a cumulative exam to come up, we would take a little time each week to practice problems I had previously learned how to do. This helped ensure that I didn't get rusty and lose those skills I had already practiced.

Lastly, Mr. Rogo took the time to preview concepts that were coming up in class in the week ahead. This made it so much easier for me to pay attention in class. Imagine two fifth-graders listening to a lecture on the history of Nepal. One of these kids has never heard of the country before, while the other visited Nepal last summer. Which kid will remember more of what the teacher was talking about?

Most likely, the second child will be able to remember a lot more of what the teacher said. We are much more comfortable learning about things that are already familiar, because we relate new knowledge to old knowledge.[27] Even if the second child didn't specifically study the history of Nepal while he was there, he will have images and experiences to attach to the names and events the teacher is discussing.

The same goes for subjects like math and science. Knowing ahead of time what the teacher would talk about really helped me focus during class. Instead of feeling intimidated, I felt excited because I was already ahead of the game.

How Good is Good Enough?

Just as all kids need to develop organizational skills to succeed in college and life, everyone can benefit from over-learning, reviewing and previewing. Even students who are not struggling to get good grades in middle and high school will find these techniques beneficial, especially if they go to a selective college or enter a difficult field of study.

That said, sometimes it can be tricky to decide what level of under-performance warrants parental intervention. Some parents aren't satisfied unless all their children get straight A's. While some children may rise eagerly to this standard, others may find it too much pressure.

On the other hand, a C or a D in a class may mean that the student really isn't learning enough to move on. For at least two decades, most American schools have been inflating grades. Many studies demonstrate that students are getting higher grades than in previous generations, but their SAT and ACT scores are declining.[28] This would suggest that students' improving grades do not necessarily reflect an increase in knowledge or skill level, and that a C today is more like a D or an F a generation ago.

I think it is perfectly reasonable to expect students to bring home A's and B's. If a child is getting A's and B's but you believe he is capable of getting all A's, it may be better to exercise some patience rather than insisting on a perfect report card. Give him a chance to get motivated on his own. On the other hand, if your student is really trying and still getting C's or D's, it may be time to intervene. This could mean changing the child's class placement or hiring a tutor.

My year in algebra ended well, because my parents caught the problem in time and acted promptly. If they hadn't, I would have fallen hopelessly behind. My tutor helped me catch up on all the concepts I had missed as well as make sure I was learning all the new material being presented each day. It took intense and consistent practice and a lot of extra time, especially at first, but it gave me the tools to succeed that year and beyond.

TURN IN YOUR BADGE

Supporting our kids in school often means walking that fine line between offering enough oversight and accountability without micromanaging them. This is a challenging for any parent, so don't be too hard on yourself if you struggle to strike the right balance. We all do!

One great option is to set up a weekly appointment to go over grades together. Online grade portals have made it easier than ever to keep tabs on our children's academic progress. However, some parents may find themselves checking grades every day or even multiple times a day. This leads to greater stress and often makes children feel smothered.

A set weekly appointment gives kids a chance to prove they

can handle classes on their own while enabling you to keep an eye on everything. This cuts down on power struggles between you and your child and minimizes unnecessary conflict.

When it comes to talking about a child's progress in a particular class, the same principles we've discussed in earlier chapters apply. Try not to discuss things when you're upset or stressed out. Instead, set up a time to talk together when everyone is calm.

A set weekly appointment gives kids a chance to prove they can handle classes on their own while enabling you to keep an eye on everything.

If a child has gotten a bad grade on a test, try not to dwell on it. Chances are, she already feels upset and disappointed. Instead, try asking her, "Moving forward, what do you think you can do differently?" This puts the focus in the right place.

Be sure to give your child a chance to focus on the positive. You might say something like, "Tell me how things are going in math. What do you think you are doing well?" If we only ask about the problems children are having, they will begin to have negative associations with talking to us about their schoolwork. Instead, we want to affirm their strengths just as much as we work to help them improve their weaknesses.

If a kid has a test coming up, you can always ask if the teacher gave out a study guide. (We'll talk more about how to get the most out of study guides in the next chapter!) Instead of reminding them to study, you could ask, "How do you *plan* to study?" Once again, questions like these get your child thinking, helping stimulate and strengthen executive function.

A QUICK RECAP

- There are many reasons for content struggles, including an inability to pay attention in class, a previous bad experience in a subject, and a mismatch between a teaching style and the student's learning style.

- If a student is struggling with the content of a particular class, parents must recognize it and intervene promptly.

- If a student is behind in a cumulative subject such as math or a math-based science, the intervention must be both intense and consistent to help the student catch up and succeed moving forward.

- Some content struggles are relatively short-term. Parents can help by getting the child started, asking questions that activate the executive center of the brain, or directing the child to helpful websites.

- Parents should try to strike a balance between offering their children support and enabling them to study independently.

- Rather than monitoring your child's grades continually, try setting up an appointment to view them together once a week.

- When communicating with your children about grades, try to focus on moving forward rather than expressing your frustration over past performance.

6

Study Strategies That Really Work

Like every new teacher, I began my career with the desire to help every single one of my students excel. I had just finished my master's degree, and I was very eager to put all the techniques and strategies I had learned into practice with my room full of fourth-graders.

I lovingly decorated my classroom and carefully crafted my lesson plans. I also spent hours creating detailed study guides to help my students prepare for their tests. I was so proud of how thorough I had made these guides, and I just knew if the kids would use them, they would all have great success.

As you might imagine, things turned out a little differently than I expected. When I actually graded that first stack of tests, I discovered that some students had done really well, while many others hadn't. Naturally, I assumed that the kids who did poorly just hadn't studied. But I wanted to be sure, so I decided to investigate.

I began by asking various students how they had prepared for the test. A few kids who performed well responded as I had expected: they had studied, and often their parents had used the study guide to quiz them. Then I asked a sweet little boy named Rory—who had done poorly—how much he had studied. I expected him to admit that he hadn't really tried his best.

Instead, Rory's big blue eyes welled up with tears, as he answered, "Mrs. Dolin! I studied so hard! I really, really tried! I don't know what happened!"

Of course, some of the kids who didn't do well on the test hadn't studied very much. But I found that a good number of kids were like Rory: they really had put in some significant effort and still hadn't performed well. What was going on?

STUDY STRATEGIES THAT DON'T WORK

When I created my study guides, I naively assumed that my students would know how to use them. But just like kids don't naturally know how to brush their teeth, tie their shoes, or actually take the trash out when it gets too full, they aren't born with an innate ability to study for tests. They have to be taught.

Learning By Osmosis Isn't A "Thing"

According to research published in *Education Week*,[29] 84 percent of students prepare for tests by rereading the class materials. This means they go back over their books or worksheets—which they may have highlighted or underlined—and just take in the same words over again.

The problem is that—for most students—**highlighting, underlining, and rereading** material are passive activities that bear little resemblance to the way we actually learn. There are ways to make these techniques work for short-term success on a quiz that covers very limited material, but rereading as the primary method of studying does not produce long-term comprehension or retention.

Re-reading is more than just ineffective. According to researchers at Harvard University, rereading "involves a kind of unwitting self-deception as growing familiarity with the text comes to feel like mastery of the content. The hours immersed in rereading can seem like due diligence, but the amount of study time is no measure of mastery."[30] Unfortunately, many students (and parents and teachers for that matter) actually believe this is the only way to study. Most likely, many of my fourth-graders were just staring at the study guides I gave them, hoping they would magically absorb the information and somehow reproduce it on the test, resulting in a stellar grade. And they were honestly surprised (and dismayed!) when this didn't happen.

The Crammer, The Memorizer, and The Absorber

I have also found that kids can engage in these kinds of short-sighted, passive study methods in a few different ways. The **crammer** puts off studying until the last minute. Often, he won't begin looking at the material until the night before—or even the morning of—a test. Then that surge of adrenaline will kick in, and he will try to get as much information into his head as quickly as possible.

Crammers are not just procrastinating. They often believe they are better off "learning" the information as close to the test as possible, so they will have less time to forget it. Some are successful on quizzes and other short-term evaluations, which only bolsters their commitment to their way of doing things. But as you might imagine, this method doesn't work so well for cumulative exams. (And, as we'll discuss in the last bonus chapter, in most colleges, there are *only* cumulative exams!)

In contrast, the **memorizer** doesn't necessarily put off studying until the last minute. In fact, she may plan out her studying well ahead of time. But she is much more comfortable focusing on names, dates, formulas, and other concrete facts, rather than the connections between those facts or their applications.

For example, a memorizer will have no trouble recalling the formula for distance (rate times time). But when asked to use that formula to calculate how long it takes two trains approaching one another from opposite directions to meet, she is at a loss. She may struggle with word problems, exercises that are set up differently than she is accustomed to, or "free response" essay questions. She will readily recall that the American Revolution began in 1775 and the French Revolution in 1789, but she might not be able to discuss their similarities and differences very easily.

Memorizers often have success in elementary school, but struggle in the later grades and in college, where they are expected to synthesize several ideas and articulate original thoughts.

Finally, we have the **absorber,** who often believes he doesn't need to study at all. He's so good at taking in the information when the teacher is talking—or so he believes—that he thinks he will be able to remember all of it come test day. He probably (like the crammer) did this very successfully early on, so it has become an ingrained habit. But once he's required to learn more difficult and complex concepts and skills, this method quickly falls short of producing the results he achieved previously.

The absorber approach is also closely tied with the "fixed mindset" belief system we'll talk about in Chapter 8. Because absorbers have had success with what seems to them to be a natural ability to just "know" the information they're being taught, it's even more of a blow to their self-esteem when they start to struggle. For these students, the solution to their problems may go beyond a simple change in strategy and require a change in mindset as well.

Because crammers, memorizers and absorbers experience limited success with their methods, they can become very attached to them and resist outside attempts to help them change. Fortunately, there are very simple ways to help all three kinds of children improve in their study habits and prepare for long-term success.

ADOPTING THE PRINCIPLE OF PRACTICE

Would you prepare for a road race just by studying a map of the course you had to run? What about getting ready for a violin recital by just looking at the sheet music? Of course not! But that's exactly what kids are doing when they study for tests by rereading.

At the root of the problem, far too many kids think about test preparation in very vague terms, rather than seeing it as a concrete set of tasks. This makes studying seem complicated and overly-difficult. Homework assignments usually have a straightforward beginning and ending: finish the ten problems or write out the definitions for the twenty vocabulary words.

But how do you know when you're done studying for a semester exam?

Well, how would you actually prepare for the race I just mentioned? You might run several times a week to build up your endurance. You might mix in some sprinting to build up your speed. You might walk the course ahead of time so that you didn't have to think too much about where to turn, or what path to follow on race day.

At the root of the problem, far too many kids think about test preparation in very vague terms, rather than seeing it as a concrete set of tasks.

And for the violin recital? You might prepare by actually playing the piece of music over and over, giving extra attention and repetition to the parts of the piece that give you trouble.

As it turns out, that's exactly the kind of preparation that our kids need for tests. They need a defined practice regimen that goes beyond just familiarizing them with the information. They need to practice actually doing what the test will ask them to do.

For example, to prepare for a math test, they need to work practice problems. To prepare for a Spanish test, they need to pick up a pencil and practice doing exactly what the test will require of them, whether it's conjugating verbs, translating sentences, or answering questions about a paragraph they read.

Once kids are in the mindset of practicing for a test rather than just looking over class materials, the steps they need to prepare become much clearer, the most effective of which are outlined below.

Space Out the Studying

We often think of exams as testing what we have stored in our memory, but this isn't quite true. They actually test what we can *recall* from our memory at will.

Researchers at Harvard University discovered that "[i]f learners spread out their study of a topic, returning to it periodically over time, they remember it better."[31] Just like with music and athletics, the most effective way to prepare is to distribute practice over several days instead of doing it all at the last minute. It's better to run four times a week for thirty minutes than to run once a week for two hours, because your muscles get stronger as they recover. In the same way, studying twenty minutes a day for three days is more effective than studying just an hour in one day. Because the more often we practice recalling information, the better we will be able to summon it on an exam.

You can also space out your study of a topic within a single study session by taking short breaks and switching between topics. For example, rather than studying math for an hour before dinner, chemistry for an hour after dinner and then history for an hour before bed, it can be more effective to do math problems for twenty minutes, history flashcards for twenty minutes and chemistry problems for twenty minutes, in two or three different sessions.[32]

Read Actively

Have you ever been reading a book and noticed that your mind began to wander? Your eyes could be sweeping across the pages, taking in the words, but your brain is totally focused on something else. If you were to go back and look at the pages you were reading, you probably wouldn't be able to remember much of the information contained there.

Unfortunately, kids—especially those with executive function weaknesses—often read this way. They are physically in front of their books, but their minds are all over the place. Active reading—reading intentionally for full comprehension and evaluation—takes practice and maturity.

Active reading is a skill that can be learned and improved.

Fortunately, active reading is a skill that can be learned and improved. One of the simplest strategies is to have kids pause after every page or so and ask themselves questions ("self-talk") about what they just read. If they are reading non-fiction, they might ask themselves, "What did I just learn? Why is it important? How does this fit with everything else in the chapter?" If they're reading fiction, they can ask, "What just happened? Why did the character do that? What is the author trying to communicate?" There are infinite variations on these kinds of questions that can help young readers meaningfully interact with their reading material.

Another strategy is for kids to take notes as they read. These notes can answer the questions above, or they can record important information, facts, dates, and so on. This will take longer, but they will probably retain much more of what they have read for a much longer time. The most important thing is to develop the habit of pausing periodically and considering what they have just read, whether they write it down or just think about it.

Many students also find it helpful to skim what they plan to read ahead of time, especially for non-fiction. This is a version of the "previewing" we talked about in the last chapter. By giving their brains a heads-up on what to expect, they make it easier to store and recall new information. After they are done reading, writing a short summary of the material (and then reviewing that summary later) is also a very effective way to retain and recall information.

Make the Most of the Study Guide

As I mentioned at the beginning of this chapter, many of my students would automatically take the study guide home and re-read it. Not only was this review passive instead of active, it was a really inefficient use of their study time. They were studying *everything* on the guide, instead of focusing on the parts that were giving them trouble.

I also discovered that many of the students who did well had parents who would get involved in their studying, engaging them with the material and asking them questions about it. But of course, not every child has parents who are able to do that, so I decided to teach all my kids how to take full advantage of their study guides on their own.

The first thing I did was hand out three copies of the study guide to each student. (This is rarely necessary now that study guides can be posted on homework portals or distributed by other electronic methods.) We would complete most of the first copy in class. Then I instructed them to go home and fill out as much of the second study guide as they could without looking at the answers. Once they got stuck, they could look at the first study guide and fill in the rest.

The second night, they could take the third blank study guide and repeat the process. At this point, they would be able to fill in almost all the answers on their own. Any answers they didn't remember, they could then spend extra time studying.

After teaching this method of studying, I finally handed out the tests. I watched anxiously as my students wrote furiously with their pencils. To my delight, the results were much better. This method worked amazingly well, and all my students who employed it saw their performance improve.

Of course, not every child took advantage of the new strategy, but those who did were able to excel even without the direct help of a parent. I knew I had given them a technique that would serve them well for the rest of their lives.

As kids get older in high school and college, it is of course possible that not every teacher will give out a study guide for a test. Even in those cases, however, teachers should give students some idea about the scope of material that the test will cover. Students can then create their own study guides and practice tests by looking at those sections of the text book, discussion questions, and class notes. They should ask themselves what questions they think the teacher might ask and try to answer them. For tests in math or science, they should try to rework homework problems multiple times. The overall method of study—focusing on recalling important facts and ideas—will work with or without a study guide.

PRACTICAL STRATEGIES TO LEARN MORE IN LESS TIME

In addition to the guiding principle of "practice" we just discussed, there are several practical strategies you can use to increase the efficiency and effectiveness of your kids' study time:

1. **Distributed Practice** Studies show that when students use a concept called Distributed Practice, or Spaced Practice, as compared with Massed Practice, as discussed by Peter Brown, Henry Roediger, and Mark McDaniel in their book, *Make it Stick: The Science of Successful Learning*,[33] they are far more likely to do better on tests. For example, if your child has a test on Friday, he could study for an hour on Thursday night, but he would actually get a better grade if he took the same amount of time and distributed it over multiple days—20 minutes Tuesday, 20 on Wednesday, and 20 on Thursday. The reason he'll get a better grade is not because he's reviewed the material multiple times; it's that he's slept on it. When you learn information and then sleep on it, you're consolidating that information into long-term memory. However, when you cram for a test, that information is learned at a superficial level, really for regurgitation the next day. It's going into short-term memory. Long-term memory is more beneficial, because when you have a

test later on, say a month later, you're much more likely to be able to retrieve it.

2. **Utilize Multi-Modal Practice** In the last chapter, I introduced the idea of different learning styles: auditory, visual, and kinesthetic. Although students may prefer one way of learning over the others, we actually learn most effectively when we can employ all three modalities. Multi-modal practice engages the brain in many different ways, helping students comprehend more deeply and recall information more quickly and accurately.

   There are several ways to do this. Students can make up flashcards to study visually, but they can also quiz and be quizzed by a parent or another student, employing the auditory component. Writing out the information utilizes a tactile method. The more students can study in a variety of ways, the better they will learn.

3. **Teach it Back** The Roman philosopher Seneca famously observed that "While we teach, we learn." One of the best ways to learn is to explain information to someone else. In my tutoring practice, tutors generally use a 5 to 1 ratio for instruction and "teach back," meaning that after every five minutes they spend teaching, they will have students spend one minute explaining the material back to them. This is the method my math tutor used with me back in eighth grade, and it is extremely helpful for kids whose minds tend to wander in class.

4. **Study in a Group** Students often learn more enthusiastically from one another. They can go over study guides together, asking each other questions and taking the

opportunity to teach back the material to each other. This can be done in person or by video chat over FaceTime or Skype. Of course, a large study group may not be the most effective, since it can be very easy to lose focus and simply socialize. A group of two to three students may be most effective.

5. **Study Before Completing Assignments** When kids put studying for a quiz or test last on their list of things to do, they tend to cut it short or neglect it altogether. If your child has a French verb worksheet and some math problems due tomorrow and a history test in three days, it may make the most sense for her to study for the history test first and then tackle the rest of her homework.

6. **Schedule Strategically** Dan Pink's book *When: The Scientific Secrets of Perfect Timing* (mentioned in Chapter 2) explains which times of the day are optimal for different kinds of tasks. He suggests we do best with analytical work during our peak (morning), administrative work during our trough (afternoon), and creative work during our recovery (late afternoon/early evening).

   Although we don't have control over our kids' schedules while they are in school, we can help them plan their tasks strategically after school (or add in a short break as suggested in Chapter 2) and on the weekends. Analytical tasks might include assignments in math and science. Administrative tasks could involve organizing their binders and notebooks, keeping their assignment book up to date, or making sure their study space is clean. Finally, writing papers, responding to literature, or working on a project or presentation utilizes more creativity and fits well into the "recovery" phase.

7. **Review Right Before Bed** We don't often think of sleep as a study aid, but it really is. Reviewing select pieces of information right before bed is another great way to help lock them get into our long-term memory. A study at MIT confirmed that people who napped after memorizing certain information remembered more of it than those who did not nap.[34]

8. **Utilize Study Apps** Once again, software engineers have developed some great applications to aid in learning and retention. *Quizlet* enables students to create their own electronic flashcards and will generate different kinds of practice quizzes and matching games to help them study. *Evernote* is an organizational tool to help students keep track of class notes, research, and other information with the ability to synch across devices. *Study Blue* connects students who want to study collaboratively, enabling them to share notes, study guides, and flashcards with each other. *GoConqr* works great for visual learners, providing tools to create mind maps of various topics, as well as track how much they are learning.

9. **Use Music with Caution** Does music really help kids study, as some of them insist? Or is it an unhelpful distraction? The answer is somewhat mixed. Music can be very effective for putting us in a better mood, which does indeed help us study better. But it can also distract kids from their work, dividing their attention between their assignments and the music itself.

Some kids are very sensitive to noise and really need to study in an area that is as quiet as possible. But other kids who better tolerate background noise can still get caught up listening to lyrics instead of focusing on their work. Just as often, kids begin playing DJ on their phones, skipping around until they find the song or playlist they want.

A great compromise can be making a **study playlist** with music they enjoy but preferably without lyrics. This could include instrumental versions of songs they know, or the scores of movies that they like. A playlist of a certain length can double as a timer if they are going over material for a set amount of time. Students can start the playlist, and then place the phone out of reach, so it isn't a visual distraction anymore.

10. **Personalize the Support** Crammers will improve a great deal when they learn the benefit of spacing out their studying with distributed practice. It may help to show them how they really won't be spending more time on a subject, just distributing that time differently and reaping greater rewards. Crammers also like to use those weird windows of time—on the bus, before practice or waiting in the doctor's office—to get some of their studying done.

Memorizers often show greatest improvement from utilizing active reading techniques such as asking themselves questions as they read. They will also benefit from multi-modal learning and studying with friends. All these strategies help them engage with the material in a more comprehensive way, deepening their understanding and retention.

Absorbers often don't believe they need to study at all, so they are honestly surprised when they see things on the test they don't remember with absolute clarity. When you help them make the most of the study guide, they have a chance to identify their weaknesses and focus on them.

TURN IN YOUR BADGE

One of the toughest things to learn as a parent is how to be proactive rather than reactive. Life is busy and moves so quickly. It's very hard to find time to plan, and so we often find ourselves responding to events in the heat of the moment:

> *"You didn't start studying yet!?*
>
> *"Don't you have a test tomorrow?"*
>
> *"You hardly studied at all yesterday! No wonder you got a C!"*
>
> *"Put down that phone or I'm taking it away!"*

But the best way to communicate with our kids about studying is to work as hard as we can to stay ahead of the game. Reminders about studying work way better if they come three or four days before the test instead of the night before! And of course, we can do our best to ask **powerful questions** that get those executive functions working instead of just nagging them or telling them what to do:

> *"What's the first thing you can do to get ready for your science test?"*
>
> *"What's your strategy to prepare for your history test on Friday?"*
>
> *"On a scale of 1 to 10, how prepared do you feel for this test?"*
>
> *"What parts of the study guide do you think you should focus on?"*

Lastly, patience is a virtue. Kids learn study skills over years, not days or weeks. Consistent, incremental practice is very powerful over the long term and can help give them the tools to succeed in the future.

A QUICK RECAP

- The overwhelming majority of kids study by rereading material with no clear strategy. This is not the most efficient or effective way to prepare for a test.

- Kids with short-sighted study methods can often be categorized as crammers, memorizers, and absorbers. Crammers wait until the last minute, memorizers focus on concrete facts, and absorbers rely on intuition.

- Students need to practice doing the same kind of exercises that the test will require them to do.

- Studying should be distributed over multiple days whenever possible. Studying 20 minutes a day for three days is far more effective than studying for one hour the day before the test.

- Active reading enables students to learn much more effectively.

- Using study guides as practice tests on at least three separate occasions will greatly improve performance on exams.

- Crammers benefit most from distributed practice, memorizers from active reading, multimodal learning, and group study, and absorbers from making effective use of their study guides.

- Try to communicate as proactively as possible with your children about test preparation, asking powerful questions instead of nagging and criticizing.

7

Tackling Anxiety: Procrastination's Partner in Crime

"I don't want to go to school tomorrow. I can't take this test!" Tommy insisted.

"What are you talking about?" his mother asked cheerily. "You already studied a lot. You'll be fine!"

"No, I can't do it. Please don't make me go," he begged.

"Honey, calm down. You're getting all worked up over nothing! Just relax and try your best. Everything will be fine, you'll see!"

To Tommy's mother, getting worked up over a test you've already prepared for seems like a bit of an overreaction. After all, in the grand scheme of things (to her at least), one little test is a "drop in the bucket" compared to an ocean of real world problems like earning a living, taking care of elderly parents, and keeping everyone in the family fed, healthy, and happy. Something so trivial is hardly worth putting up such a fight over.

To Tommy though, his science test is right up there among the most momentous, pressure-packed, stress-inducing events in his life, competing neck-and-neck with getting picked early enough in the order for kickball, and awaiting an answer from his first real middle school crush about whether she'll be attending the fall dance and might consider standing close to him. So to him, her words are not only frustratingly "out of touch," but may also make the problem even worse. And in the battle against procrastination, with grades and self-confidence hanging in the balance, anxiety can be a crippling force with which to contend.

WHAT IS ANXIETY? A NATURAL RESPONSE TURNED CHRONIC

Everyone gets nervous or worried now and then. Sometimes, a little nervous energy can actually jump start our engines and help us prepare effectively for something important: a test, an interview, or a speech. But for kids like Tommy, that nervous energy becomes an overwhelming, ever-present sense of dread. He feels like something terrible is about to happen, and he feels powerless to stop it.

At its core, a problematic level of anxiety reflects a distorted understanding of the world around us. Anxiety causes our brains to perceive certain normal parts of life—going to school, taking a test, meeting new people—as dangerous or threatening. It can cause children to see their entire lives in stark black and white terms: *"If I can't get an A, I might as well get an F,"* or *"I don't understand how to do this problem, so that means I'm bad at math."*

Anxiety can also cause us to catastrophize, analyzing events by jumping immediately to the worst possible conclusion: *"I got a C on this Spanish test. I'm not going to get into college,"* or *"Only*

At its core, a problematic level of anxiety reflects a distorted understanding of the world around us. Anxiety causes our brains to perceive certain normal parts of life—going to school, taking a test, meeting new people—as dangerous or threatening.

100 people liked my Instagram post. Everyone at school thinks I'm ugly." Of course, these statements are silly, but just telling kids not to feel the way they are feeling doesn't usually work.

Children and teenagers may not necessarily realize they are feeling anxious. They may think they feel angry, tired, or sick. And even if they realize they are anxious, they may not be eager to talk about it (and who can blame them?) As parents, we're left with reading between the lines, on the lookout for symptoms if we suspect something might be wrong, not exactly an easy assignment.

The problem is, anxiety can snowball unless kids have the proper strategies to deal with it. This is especially true when they are thrown into unfamiliar territory or particularly stressful circumstances. Physical symptoms of anxiety include headaches, stomach aches, nausea, sweating, trembling, dizziness, fatigue and even rashes or hives. Emotional symptoms include tension, fear, irritability, frustration, and difficulty concentrating. And all of this interferes with learning, development, and proper engagement with the world.

Nearly a third of all American adolescents are estimated to have a diagnosable anxiety disorder,[35] but 80 percent of these children are not getting any treatment.[36] There are many complicated reasons for these trends, and this chapter will not cover them exhaustively. Instead, we will talk about simple steps parents can take to get their children to talk about their anxious feelings and bring them under control. We'll also talk about when to consult a professional.

I am indebted to two colleagues of mine, psychologist Dr. Maria Zimmitti, PhD and Cathi Cohen, Licensed Clinical Social Worker, who generously agreed to be interviewed on these issues.[37]

Stress vs. Anxiety: What's the difference?

Let's take a step back and define some terms. We often use the words "stress" and "anxiety" interchangeably, but they don't mean quite the same thing. In the simplest terms, stress is a reaction of the brain and body to external factors or "stressors," while anxiety is a more chronic condition.

Life is naturally full of stressors, from daily events like morning traffic and overcrowded schedules, to unusual occurrences

---

Stress is a reaction of the brain and body to external factors or "stressors," while anxiety is a more chronic condition.

---

like a family illness or accident. Our bodies respond to these events by raising our heart rates and blood pressure and releasing stress hormones, such as adrenaline and cortisol, into the blood stream.

This reaction is the "fight or flight" response you probably remember learning about in school, which enabled our ancestors to react quickly, without thinking, when faced with a dangerous predator. At the time, this was critical for our survival; however, because morning traffic or computer issues don't typically require a serious physical response, we don't use up the stress hormones in our bloodstream. This can leave us feeling agitated if we don't find a way to release all that nervous energy.

Even so, under normal conditions, when the stressor goes away, the stressed-out person feels better. His blood pressure and heartrate lower, his frantic thought patterns subside, and his death-grip on the steering wheel decreases. For some people, however, that "alerted" state persists, and the tension-filled sensations we just described continue, regardless of what is going on in their lives. Cohen explains that it's almost like the brain can't find the "off switch" for the stress response. That's what we call anxiety, and it can range from mild to almost crippling.

Anxiety and Executive Function

We've all had the experience of being so worried about something that we felt like we couldn't think straight. So it should come as no surprise that anxiety has a negative effect on every component of executive function that we discussed in Chapter 1.[38] The more anxious we feel, the less we are able to focus, the harder we find it to plan ahead, and the more difficult it is to remember what we've been told.

The same goes for children. Zimmitti explains that anxiety hijacks executive function, often mimicking the symptoms of ADHD. Anxious kids are distracted and have trouble processing and recalling information, because they simply can't access the executive processes to do so. For children with executive function weaknesses, anxiety can make symptoms even worse.

Where does anxiety come from?

As I mentioned, the stress response is an integral part of life. Anxiety isn't. Kids can feel anxious for all sorts of reasons, but here are a few of the most common:

1. **Transition** Any kind of transition can cause anxiety, even in children who are normally relaxed and carefree. These could be neutral transitions such as moving or transferring to a new school, a happy event like the birth of a sibling, or a distressing change like a divorce or the death of a loved one.

2. **Subject-Specific Anxiety** Children can also develop subject-specific academic anxieties, with math anxiety being one of the most commonly reported. These can be related to a specific negative experience in the subject or previous poor performance. Children can also pick up these anxieties from the adults in their lives. For example, children whose elementary school teachers were anxious about teaching math or whose parents suffered from math anxiety are more

likely to have math anxiety themselves.[39] In short, kids are very good at reading social cues from the adults in their lives. If our body language and emotions communicate that something like math is difficult or should be dreaded, our kids are more likely to feel anxious in response.

3. **Lack of sufficient sleep** Not getting enough sleep leads to physical symptoms associated with anxiety such as headaches, nausea, and hyperactivity, and it also makes the emotional symptoms of anxiety worse.[40] As I've already mentioned, kids and teens need a lot of sleep. Homework, extracurricular activities, and parent work schedules understandably push bedtime later, leading to sleep deprivation in children of all ages. Screen time also interferes with sleep, both because of the distraction of the screen itself, and the role of blue light in suppressing melatonin, the hormone associated with sleep regulation.[41]

4. **Overscheduling** Even if kids are getting enough sleep, overscheduling can cause stress and anxiety. Some kids have a lot of energy and thrive when they go from school to sports to music lessons every day. Others need more down time to play and decompress.

5. **Social Anxiety** Some children may actually be fine with the academic component of school, but they may be experiencing anxiety related to interacting with the teachers and other children. This could be social anxiety, a condition in which many different kinds of harmless, normal social interactions cause the child undue fear and dread. Or your child may be dealing with a bully or another kind of toxic environment in school.

6. **Excessive Social Media Use** Somewhat related, social media use can increase both loneliness and anxiety in users of all ages.[42] The relationship is multifaceted. First, social media use can amplify the normal anxieties that kids feel about fitting in and social standing at school. Second, cyber-bullying or shaming means that sometimes school drama follows kids home, making it feel all-encompassing.

   While many healthy kids use social media in moderation, some do not readily understand that the images they see on Facebook or Instagram are carefully chosen by users. They begin to think that everyone else's lives are somehow more exciting or glamorous than theirs, or they may feel hurt when they see postings about an event that they were not invited to. They may even feel rejected if their own posts do not receive as much positive attention as they had hoped.

7. **Inherited Anxious Tendencies** Of course, some kids are naturally more anxious than others. Cohen explains that some components of anxiety appear to be genetic, while others are shaped by environment. If you or your spouse struggle with anxiety, don't be surprised if it shows up in your kids.

Some of these causes of anxiety have relatively straightforward solutions. For example, a quick intervention for insufficient sleep is an earlier bedtime, and it may be worth giving up an extracurricular activity or another obligation to make this possible. Many families guard against excessive electronics and social media use by setting up a charging station where children are asked to put their devices at a certain time each night.

Other causes of anxiety are more complex, uncontrollable, and intertwined with multiple aspects of your child's life. For example, a transition to a new school may cause some acute anxiety towards the classroom, which results in a lapse in attention. This might snowball into more chronic subject-specific anxiety and loss of confidence when the child comes home with a "D" on a first exam because he or she didn't understand much of the unit that was covered. Here, the solution is not so simple, and requires thoughtful engagement with the problem and the formulation of a strategy to get the child back on track. Keep these causes in mind as we discuss how to address anxiety-related procrastination in the following section.

HELPING YOUR CHILD OVERCOME ANXIETY-RELATED PROCRASTINATION

When faced with an anxious child, we can be tempted as parents to simply help the child avoid the source of his or her anxiety. That's not to say that there aren't times when this makes sense. If your kindergartener is exhausted and the clown at the birthday party frightens her, there is no reason she has to overcome that particular fear that day. In fact, pushing her too much when she doesn't have the resources or framework to address her anxiety is almost guaranteed to make matters worse. Anxiety tends to feed on itself in the moment.

But suppose she is afraid of dogs. You may not have a dog, but maybe several of her cousins and friends do. One way to handle her fear is to enable her to avoid all contact with dogs. You could refuse to visit houses with dogs, or you might call ahead and ask the family to put the dog in a cage or in the backyard before you come over.

While this strategy avoids the immediate negative reaction from your child, it will probably make her phobia of dogs worse in the future. Accommodating an anxiety in the long-term reinforces the idea that the object of fear presents a real threat. Each time she avoids contact with a dog, it affirms the idea that she is safe because she is away from what she fears. Only when she has the experience of being safe in the presence of a dog is she likely to revise her belief that all dogs are dangerous. Kids need the chance to prove their anxious thoughts wrong if they are to overcome them.

The same principle applies to fear of rejection at a dance, worries over making varsity soccer, or any school-related anxiety. Cohen points out that avoiding schoolwork because of anxiety can become a self-fulfilling prophecy. Anxious students put off their work because they are afraid they cannot do it perfectly or they can't learn what they need to know for the test. When they finally do get started, they don't have enough time to do a good job or to adequately study the material.

Avoiding schoolwork because of anxiety can become a self-fulfilling prophecy.

But there are several simple steps you can take to help your kids face their schoolwork-related fears and eventually overcome them:

Naming the Fear

"Tommy, what are you afraid of?" his mother asked, trying a different approach to get to the bottom of his feelings.

For mild anxiety, simply talking about the feelings may be enough to help children get going.

"I'm afraid that I'll fail the test."

"Well, what have you done to prepare?" she asked matter-of-factly.

"Well . . ." Tommy said, thinking it over. "I read and outlined both chapters. And then I answered all the questions at the end."

"Well, it sounds like you're pretty prepared to me," his mother replied, "but even if you did fail, what's the worst thing that would happen?"

One of the most important tools for overcoming anxiety is to help your children develop a greater awareness of how they are feeling and why. Sometimes, just being able to articulate, "I'm worried about my test tomorrow," goes a long way toward diffusing the tension your child is feeling.

For mild anxiety, simply talking about the feelings may be enough to help children get going. Once they say things out loud, they may realize how misplaced or even silly the fear is. It's when the feelings stay bottled up inside that they become so overwhelming.

Cohen likes to teach kids to become detectives with their own thoughts and feelings. If a pre-schooler is afraid that there is monster under the bed, sometimes the most powerful solution is shining a flashlight under the bed and showing her there is nothing there (except maybe some toys she forgot to put away!) With older children who are afraid of getting bad grades or not getting into college, sometimes talking directly about those thoughts is the best way to prevent them from having power.

Tommy's mom knew he had already studied enough, but instead of just telling him that, she asked him to think about it. This got his mind working a little more logically, instead of being overwhelmed by his emotions. This simple exercise was a small but significant step in teaching him to access his executive functions and take control of his feelings on his own.

Overcoming the Pull of Perfectionism

Tommy struggles to start his work because he wants to do it perfectly. In first and second grade, this wasn't too much of an issue. But now that he is getting older, his perfectionist tendencies are causing real problems.

As a parent, it's tempting to tolerate perfectionism in the early years, because it may seem to get kids to perform better in school. After all, what could possibly be wrong with them wanting to do everything right? But as students get older and schoolwork gets more difficult, perfectionism often becomes more about avoiding mistakes than high achievement. As we'll discuss in the next chapter, this can lead children to look for easy tasks they can do perfectly rather than taking on the kinds of challenges that will ultimately help them learn and grow.

In some kids, perfectionism can become toxic. They torture themselves for every mistake, convinced that they are unworthy of love or approval if they do even one tiny thing wrong. Zimmitti often sees previously functional perfectionists crash and burn their junior or senior year of high school, when they are facing both challenging classes and the pressure of applying to college.

Try to teach your kids that making mistakes is a normal part of being human. Share some of your own mistakes with your kids, and show them how everything ended up fine. And be sure to let them know that you don't expect or demand perfection from them or from yourself.

In some kids, perfectionism can become toxic. They torture themselves for every mistake, convinced that they are unworthy of love or approval if they do even one tiny thing wrong.

Prioritizing the Anxiety Away

Sometimes children will feel overwhelmed by all the work they think they have to do. As I mentioned in Chapter 5, getting anxious children started with a small task—a few math problems or a couple of spelling exercises—can help them get the engine going. But anxious kids, especially as they get older, may also need a little extra help organizing their study time.

Often, kids who deal with school-related anxiety aren't naturally able to prioritize their work. They have trouble thinking through what needs to be done when, and they struggle to break down bigger projects into manageable pieces. In this case, helping your children think through which tasks are most important can help dispel their anxiety and empower them to finish.

Try sitting down with your child and writing out everything she has to do. When she's feeling anxious, she may feel like everything on the list is absolutely urgent. But most likely, there are some things that are urgent, some things that are important, and other things that could be put off or even not done at all.

Try sitting down with your child and writing out everything she has to do.

Help her sort each of her tasks into three categories: things she "Must Do," things she "Should Do" and things she "Could Do."

- **Must Do** items absolutely have to get done that day. These include important assignments due the following day or studying for a test the next day.

- **Should Do** items are helpful to do or at least start, such as getting a head start studying for a test later in the week or working on a long-term project. These are good ideas, but if she has a lot of other work due the next day, maybe they could be put off.

- **Could Do** items are tasks that may be recommended but are not required. They could include extra-credit assignments, suggested reading, and other extra work. Activities like these can be a good idea, but if the child has a busy week, they can easily be put aside.

Watch out for Over-Studying!

Over-studying can be a counter-intuitive problem for parents. Kids like Kyle (the Bright But Disorganized student from our previous chapters) have never over-studied a day in their lives. In fact, the minute they show signs of motivation to put in more effort than is required, we should strongly encourage and affirm them.

But perfectionists like Tommy will often pressure themselves to over-study, spending significantly more time on a subject than is reasonable for the type of test or their grade level. They believe if they can just put in enough time with the material, they will protect themselves from getting anything wrong. Cohen sees this as the "fight" side of the fight-or-flight response: the child is "fighting" with the "threat" of the test by overdoing his or her preparation.

But this strategy doesn't usually help kids like Tommy perform better for several reasons. First, it is hard to learn or remember things well when we are feeling anxious, because as mentioned previously, anxiety hijacks our executive functions. Second, anxious kids are not necessarily using their time well when they are studying. They are probably rereading or using other ineffective methods as we discussed in the last chapter. Third, Zimmitti reminds us that over-studiers may stay up too late, cutting into sleep time, which will make the anxiety worse and likely hurt performance as well.

If you think your child may be prone to over-studying, try to help him understand that the world will not end if he doesn't get a perfect grade. Assure him that he doesn't need to go over every single detail for his test. Remind him about how important sleep is, and encourage him to get to bed on time.

If you think your child may be prone to over-studying, try to help him understand that the world will not end if he doesn't get a perfect grade.

When to See a Professional

As I've said, a little anxiety in children is normal. All kinds of young kids are afraid of the dark, get worried when they are separated from their parents, or are reluctant to be in new environments and try new things. If a child shows signs of these behaviors during the preschool years, or if his anxiety is just causing him to get a few B's instead of A's, it is quite likely that he will grow out of it on his own.

For older children, getting nervous for a test or a big game or performance is also completely normal, as is dealing with an excess of stress stemming from uncomfortable situations in their social lives. These types of anxiety are part and parcel of growing up and can usually be handled, if not by your child on her own, with a little guidance from Mom and Dad.

However, there are times when it may be best to take your child to a professional therapist. According to Zimmitti and Cohen, these include, but are not limited to, when:

1. Anxiety interferes with your child's ability to function in daily life

2. Anxiety interferes with your child's eating and/or sleeping

3. Your child refuses to go to school[43]

4. Your child has difficulty forming friendships or consistently chooses to stay home rather than socialize with friends

5. Anxiety is significantly affecting your child's performance in school

6. Symptoms are severe or unrelenting

7. Symptoms do not respond to your efforts to help at home

8. Your child shows signs of depression or self-harm

If you aren't quite sure about where your child's symptoms fall on the spectrum of anxiety, there is really no harm in seeing a therapist to be on the safe side. Zimmitti observes that while not every anxious child develops into an anxious adolescent or adult, almost every anxious adolescent showed signs of unusual levels of anxiety in earlier childhood. Earlier intervention can help anxious children learn coping mechanisms and possibly prevent their symptoms from persisting into adulthood.

The good news is that even severe anxiety is extremely treatable, with or without medication. Cognitive behavioral therapy in particular has a very high rate of success. The sooner you begin addressing anxiety symptoms, the sooner your child can build up an arsenal of skills to help him overcome it.

If you aren't quite sure about where your child's symptoms fall on the spectrum of anxiety, there is really no harm in seeing a therapist to be on the safe side.

PRACTICAL STRATEGIES FOR
TEST TAKING ANXIETY

At the outset of this chapter, Tommy expressed a not-so-un-common resistance to one situation in particular: taking a test. And as you're probably acutely aware already, the circumstances that surround test taking are prime for generating anxiety. Time pressure, being put on the spot, and fear of failure all combine to create a "perfect storm" for a child unprepared to handle the demands.

It is completely normal to feel a little nervous before an exam, especially a high-stakes test like the SAT. However, if the feeling of nervousness causes your child's mind to go blank and interferes with his performance, he may have test anxiety. As mentioned above, if the anxiety is enough to make him physically ill or refuse to take the test, you may want to consult a professional therapist. But there are many simple techniques children can learn to help them cope with and overcome test anxiety.

Name the Fear

Just like with anxiety-related procrastination, sometimes teaching a child to name his fears can dispel their power. Just learning to say, "I'm afraid if I don't get a 95 on this test, I won't get an A in the class," helps the child remember that not getting an A in a class is not the end of the world.

Kids can use a piece of paper or a journal to jot down all these fears just before test time, and then put the journal away. (You may want to speak to the teacher so he or she is aware that your child will be using this technique.) Studies have shown that putting feelings down on paper helps anxious children release the tension and allows them to concentrate just as well as their non-anxious peers.[44]

Do a Brain Dump

Sometimes kids become anxious about trying to remember every formula, date, or irregular verb before their test. This can cause their minds to go blank when they receive their test papers. It can also prompt them to rush through a test, skimming items instead of reading carefully and thinking through their answers. They want to finish as quickly as possible out of fear that they will forget what they have studied.

Of course, the distributed practice mentioned in the last chapter can really help with this anxiety, because it gives kids more experience recalling the information from their memories. But another great idea for these kids is to have them quickly write out all the information they are afraid of forgetting as soon as they received their test paper. This relieves the immediate fear that they will forget the information and enables them to concentrate on reading each question carefully and completing it.

Breathing Techniques

Sometimes kids need help combating the physical symptoms of anxiety. This can be true for kids who are visibly affected by anxiety and for those who may seem emotionally fine, but still find themselves sweating or having their hearts beat faster before a test. This is where simple breathing techniques can make a huge difference.

Breathing is involuntary, which is a good thing, since we wouldn't want to forget to do it. When we become anxious, however, our breathing becomes shallow and rapid to prepare to fight or flee from a threat. By taking control of our breathing during these times, we are able to slow down this physiological response and bring it under our control.

Breathing techniques don't have to be complicated. I like to teach kids to "box breathe," which is simply inhaling for four seconds, holding the breath for four seconds, exhaling for four seconds, and holding the exhale for four seconds. Just doing this two or three times is often enough to bring mild anxiety under control.

Another easy technique is one-nostril breathing. This is exactly what it sounds like: just plug one nostril and breathe in and out of the other. This makes it impossible to breathe rapidly and can help even very young children halt the anxiety response.

Some kids benefit from "feather breathing." Kids can pretend they have an imaginary feather on top of their hand in front of their mouths. They breathe gently, so they don't dislodge this imaginary feather. This also prevents the rapid, intense breathing that triggers the rest of the stress/panic response.

TURN IN YOUR BADGE

When helping your child work through anxiety, it can be very helpful to take an honest look at your own experiences. If you have never dealt with anxiety yourself, you may find it very difficult to understand why your child seems so upset over nothing. You may feel like she just needs to get over her fears or grow up.

But in reality, it may be much harder for your child to do this than you imagine. Chances are, if she could find the "switch" for her anxiety, she would have turned it off by now. So, focus instead on giving her the tools to lessen and ultimately take control of her anxiety.

Parents also need to temper their reactions to mediocre or bad grades. Zimmitti reminds us that we want to be the ones our kids can come to about struggles in school, not the ones they are afraid to tell. Cohen encourages us to not only think about the standards we set for our children, but also what we model in our own lives. Do we demand only the best from ourselves or beat ourselves up when we make a mistake? Our kids are bound to pick up on this.

That said, some parents may feel as if they are walking on egg shells when dealing with an anxious child. They are afraid that they will say something that makes the child feel worse, so they don't say anything at all. When you communicate with your children about their anxieties, you want to make it clear that you understand and empathize with how they are feeling, but you also believe that they are strong and capable of overcoming their anxiety.

Kids also need to know that their parents are calm and in control of their own emotions and the situation at hand. Try to avoid fear-based questions like, *"Are you okay?" "What's wrong?"* If you ask a perfectly healthy child if she's okay enough times, she's bound to conclude there is something wrong with her!

Acknowledge how your children are feeling and utilize your **powerful questions** to help them articulate and assess their feelings: *"I've noticed you seem a little worried. Is something bothering you?" "How are you feeling about your test tomorrow?"*

Even if you aren't a naturally anxious person, all parents worry about their children now and then. You may be subconsciously allowing your own anxiety to affect not just the way you communicate with your child, but also your goals and priorities in parenting. All of us want what is best for our children, but how do we decide what is best? How do we communicate with our kids about what is important?

You may be subconsciously allowing your own anxiety to affect not just the way you communicate with your child, but also your goals and priorities in parenting.

In her 2006 book, *The Price of Privilege*, psychologist Madeline Levine explains the anxiety she sees in educated American parents this way:

> "Parents are genetically programmed to protect their children from threats. Thankfully, the more recent historical threats to our children's well-being—malnutrition and devastating childhood illnesses—have been eradicated, or greatly reduced. Yet levels of parental anxiety remain extraordinarily high . . . The perceived threats of contemporary society—competition for grades, well-known schools, prestigious job offers—should not elicit the same kinds of hyper-vigilant, controlling responses that, say, exposure to polio once elicited. Persistent worry about how well

one's child stacks up against other children inevitably leads to parents who are over-involved and emotionally exhausted as well as to children who are impaired in their ability to function independently."[45]

Schoolwork is important, but mediocre or bad grades do not present the same threat that illness and starvation once did. Choosing the right college is important, but not getting admitted to Harvard or Stanford will not prevent our children from being successful. In the next chapter, we'll look at how to keep schoolwork and grades in a healthy, balanced perspective.

A QUICK RECAP

- Anxiety is a chronic condition that hijacks executive function and has many possible sources.

- Anxiety-related procrastination can often be remedied by naming fears, confronting perfectionist tendencies, and helping children prioritize their tasks.

- Test taking anxiety can often be overcome by naming fears, doing a "brain dump" at the beginning of the test, and utilizing breathing techniques.

- Whenever your child's anxiety seems abnormal or persistent, consult a professional therapist.

- Be sure to think about your own anxiety (or lack thereof) when communicating with your anxious children about their struggles.

- Powerful questions can help your children access their executive functions and take control of their anxiety.

8

Keeping it all in Perspective

"I just don't know what I'm doing wrong!"

Those were the words of "Catherine," a frustrated mother who approached me after one of the many seminars I conduct for parents and educators. She explained that her fifth grade son was capable but unmotivated. His grades were mediocre and a constant source of conflict in the family.

Catherine was tired of fighting and desperate for a solution. Her son had always wanted to go to Disney World, so during the third quarter of the year, Catherine made her son an offer. If he could get straight A's, she would reward him by taking the entire family to the Magic Kingdom. His reaction was just what she had hoped: he was elated and promised to do better than ever at school.

For the first week, Catherine's son did exactly what he promised. He rushed home from school, opened his books and got his work done as quickly and carefully as possible. But the following week, his enthusiasm began to wane. And by the end of the month, he was back to his old ways, starting homework at the last minute and doing it half-heartedly.

Not only did Catherine's reward fail to produce the long-term behavior change she was hoping for, but she also faced an impossible dilemma over their family vacation. Should she cancel the vacation and bitterly disappoint everyone? Or should she risk teaching her son that he would get his reward regardless of what he did?

Catherine simply wanted what I think all parents do: for her son to start his homework without being told and finish it without a fight. Ultimately, she wanted him to become an independent learner, taking care of his responsibilities and getting good grades on his own because he wanted to, not because anyone was making him. But—as most of us have experienced at one time or another—her strategy didn't work as well as she had hoped.

The skills to move past procrastination are many of the same skills kids need to be successful in life. And getting kids to do anything that doesn't come naturally will almost always involve a certain degree of conflict. But we want to teach these skills in a way that develops character and nurtures—instead of strains—our relationships with our children, because that relationship will still be there long after the grades are forgotten.

The skills to move past procrastination are many of the same skills kids need to be successful in life.

WHY WE FIGHT ABOUT SCHOOL

There are some kids who are completely self-motivated and drive themselves to high levels of academic achievement without any pressure from their parents. But most kids aren't like that. And I'm guessing at least one of yours isn't either, because otherwise you probably wouldn't have picked up this book. Self-motivated kids are the exception not the rule, so it's pretty safe to say that most of us will fight with at least one of our kids about grades at some point.

So how do we prevent our relationships with our kids from becoming dominated by academics? Throughout this book, we've talked about different sources of schoolwork-related arguments. Keeping these in mind can help us minimize unnecessary conflict and keep everything in perspective.

Conflicting Time Horizons

Catherine wanted to use the reward of a Disney vacation to motivate her son to work harder in school. And research shows that rewards *can* work as motivators for kids, but only under certain conditions. Harvard University's Roland Fryer spent 6.3 million dollars to reward 38,000 kids in 261 schools for accomplishing various goals and studied how well the rewards worked. These goals included everything from reading books and doing homework, to getting good grades on quarterly report cards and achieving high standardized test scores. Kids were offered relatively small amounts of money for accomplishing these goals, and researchers recorded who followed through and who didn't.

Fryer found that the rewards worked very well for simple,

short-term goals like going to class and completing homework, but they did not work for long-term goals like a good report card or higher SAT scores.[46] He also found that it was more effective to pay kids to do their work or study rather than to get particular results on tests or quizzes, which we'll talk about more later on.

For Catherine's son, the nine weeks it would take to accomplish the goal of straight A's on a report card was simply too long a time horizon for him to manage. (As we discussed in Chapter 4, even kids with well-developed time horizons have difficulty planning more than a week or two ahead at this age.) Instead of a simple, straightforward task with a quick reward, the straight A report card involved hundreds, if not thousands, of little decisions made over months. That was just too overwhelming for a fifth-grader. After a week of trying, Catherine's son decided it just wasn't worth it.

Conflicting Priorities

Almost every parent has walked into a kid's messy bedroom and asked, "How can anyone live like this?" To most adults (and a select number of children) a certain level of disorder is just intolerable. But for most kids, it's really no big deal. These differing priorities are bound to lead to conflict, which won't be completely resolved until the child matures.

The same kind of conflicting priorities can cause arguments in our discussions of schoolwork and grades. Most parents consider success in school important, while many kids are more concerned with making friends and having fun. Parents naturally think about the long-term importance of school, while kids often assume that everything will just work out somehow.

If your child doesn't seem to care about school, know that you are not alone. In fact, a declining interest and engagement in school is the norm, not the exception. According to a 2015 Gallup poll of nearly a million students, the percentage of students engaged in school drops steadily each year from 75 percent in fifth grade to 32 percent in eleventh grade.[47]

Conflicting Maturity Levels

As has been discussed throughout the book, many kids have difficulty directing their attention to certain activities, even when they want to. This can be because of ADHD, executive function weaknesses, or simple immaturity. And besides, all kids are by definition less mature than adults. As a parent though, it's all too easy to forget this.

Because of the lack of maturity present in most kids, their desires often end up in direct conflict with their responsibilities. They want to be independent in their decision making but are still dependent on others for cash (namely, Mom and Dad, who may have other ideas about those decisions). They want to be relaxed about their responsibilities, but they still want all the benefits that come with being responsible. And for school in particular, this often means they resist working hard on homework, projects, and studying, while still expecting the ideal future that comes with academic achievement. This is very frustrating for parents, but it is not unusual or abnormal.

As we've covered, the motivation to work hard is triggered by the pleasure centers of the brain. Kids who aren't motivated for school just don't get that dopamine rush when they get their work done, so there is no built-in reason to repeat the behavior.

But motivation also changes with maturity. As they grow, young people begin to realize that their actions have consequences and begin to derive more pleasure and satisfaction from taking care of their responsibilities.

Maturity can be guided and encouraged by parents, but it cannot really be rushed. One of the best things we can do is try to remember what life was like when we were kids and give our own kids time to grow up.

Motivation also changes with maturity. As they grow, young people begin to realize that their actions have consequences and begin to derive more pleasure and satisfaction from taking care of their responsibilities.

Your Anxiety About Their Future

As discussed in the last chapter, many parents have become extremely anxious about their kids' futures. This is completely understandable. Getting into college is much more competitive than it has ever been, with schools like Stanford rejecting 96 percent of applicants and many state universities rejecting more than two thirds of those who apply.

At the same time, more kids than ever are attending and graduating from college. This means the relative value of a bachelor's degree in the job market has declined, even as college graduates continue to earn much higher incomes (on average) than those who only have a high school diploma. To add insult to injury, college costs have spiraled out of control, causing parents to worry that they may have to borrow money or deplete their savings just to give their children a decent start in life.

All this worry makes it easy to think that one bad report card is the end of the world. This in turn can lead to unnecessary arguments over grades. But there are many paths to success, and, as we'll discuss a little later, grades really aren't everything.

Vague or Unreasonable Standards

Kids need their parents to set standards for both their behavior and their performance at school. Left to their own devices, most students will not fulfill their potential or take full advantage of their educational opportunities. And there is absolutely nothing unreasonable about expecting your child to go to class, do the work that is assigned, and get reasonable grades in coursework that is appropriate for his or her abilities and interests.

But sometimes parents have expectations regarding grades or academic achievement that are simply beyond what their kids are willing or able to achieve. Some parents insist that their children take five or more AP courses each year of high school and get straight A's, punishing them severely if they don't comply. Others might demand an A on every assignment and test, not just in every class. But pushing a kid far beyond his capability or desire will probably lead to a level of frustration and conflict that is unhealthy for both the parent and the child.

In other cases, parents will say that they don't care about grades, as long as their children "try their best." But what is "their best"? Most kids don't know, and most parents, if they are honest, don't necessarily know how to clarify what they mean. Children may honestly believe they have tried their best, and parents may honestly believe they haven't. This also leads to unnecessary conflict, which we can avoid by setting clear, reasonable standards.

Communication, Communication, Communication

As discussed throughout the book, how and when you communicate with your children about school will strongly influence the amount and intensity of the conflict associated with homework and studying. Talking to your kids about grades when you are upset will never go well. Likewise, if your kids are feeling upset about a test or a class for whatever reason, it's probably best to comfort them first and discuss life lessons later when they're feeling better.

Remember that most kids—like most adults—really don't like being told what to do, especially as they get older. Resist the temptation to lecture, and instead ask powerful questions that get them thinking and planning ahead. Sometimes the best questions can be very simple. How can I help? What role would you like me to have in this process? Let your child invite you into the process, instead of taking control.

FOCUS ON THE PROCESS, NOT THE RESULTS

Catherine linked her reward of the Disney vacation to the end product she wanted: good grades. But as straightforward as grades may seem to us, they can feel mysterious to children, leading to all those unpleasant arguments. To us as parents, getting an A is a simple as doing what the teachers says. And we get frustrated when our kids can't seem to buckle down and take care of their responsibilities.

But in a kid's reality, a good grade in a class is the result of all those little processes we've talked about so far, such as managing time well, completing assignments, turning them in, and studying effectively. They don't automatically connect all those daily decisions to what they see on the report card weeks later. This is why, as the Fryer research demonstrates, rewarding the process works much better than focusing on the results, especially over the long-term.

There are several specific reasons for this:

Focusing on results leads to shortcuts

Whenever our kids think we only care about grades or a completed assignment, they will be tempted to take short cuts. For example, they may fill in random answers or write sloppy sentences just to get credit for an assignment that's being graded for completion. But once they leave school, no one will ever give them credit for doing something at a low standard just because it's done.

When parents go overboard on grades, some kids will try to get those grades by any means necessary. Unfortunately, this can lead to kids cheating, whether by using a device to look up an answer, copying off another student, or obtaining the answers to the test ahead of time. A willingness to cheat may not be limited to tests: a 2012 study revealed that 57 percent of

American teens believed that "successful people do what they have to do to win, even if it involves cheating."[48]

Even kids who do not cheat may rely too much on friends to help them get their work done or take other short cuts—like cramming—that will prevent them from learning and growing the way they should. We want our kids to know that we care a lot more about the learning process than we care about every little grade. There are many pursuits in life that don't always lead to the precise results we might have hoped for, but that doesn't mean the process isn't worthwhile.

When parents go overboard on grades, some kids will try to get those grades by any means necessary.

Focusing on the process helps kids remember the "why" and not just the "how"

Sometimes, school feels pointless to kids. But the older they get, the more they should understand how the things they are learning in school will affect their overall development as a person and be meaningful to them in the future. If we reduce the importance of school to "get good grades so you can go to a good college and get a good job," we can reinforce the idea that school is just a formality we have to endure, instead of a wonderful opportunity to learn interesting and useful things.

Of course, not everything they learn in school will relate directly to the jobs they get down the road. Kids may not use their knowledge of history in their future careers, but they will use it to be good citizens. Not everyone will use AP physics in everyday life but learning to think scientifically and mathematically can help us understand and appreciate how the world works. Learning can be a lifelong pursuit, and formal education should be its foundation, not its upward limit.

Focusing on the process will develop good habits and work ethic

Grades do matter. They matter for college and graduate school admissions and for some entry level jobs. But once a young adult advances in his career, no one will ask to see his grades anymore. Employers will be very interested, however, in the character qualities underneath the grades. Can he can get the job done? Is his work of acceptable quality? Does he work carefully? Can he meet deadlines?

Focusing on the process of studying and homework completion enables students to develop good work habits and a strong work ethic. These qualities will serve them well for the rest of their lives, regardless of where they go to college or what kinds of careers they pursue.

Learning can be a lifelong pursuit, and formal education should be its foundation, not its upward limit.

Focusing on the process helps you encourage your child's strengths

Kids who are naturally organized and on top of things get regularly rewarded for their efforts with good grades. But kids who may be deeply creative, intuitive, or analytical may not get the satisfaction of seeing their strengths show up on their report cards, especially in the early years. By focusing on the process, you can encourage and nurture these strengths that may not naturally show up on the report card.

Focusing on the process encourages intrinsic motivation

Although we all care about grades, we ultimately want our children to develop their own internal standards of excellence that will motivate them to work hard not just for a grade or a paycheck, but for the satisfaction of a job well done. This is the difference between extrinsic and intrinsic motivation, and it generally comes with time and maturity.

In his 2009 book *Drive: The Surprising Truth About What Motivates Us*, author Daniel Pink lays out the importance of three components of intrinsic motivation: autonomy, mastery, and purpose. Kids will derive a growing amount of satisfaction from their work when they feel in charge of it, see they are getting better at it, and perceive the overall purpose in it. This makes the work easier and more interesting, but it doesn't happen when we focus on grades and report cards, only when we focus on the process to get there.

Kids will derive a growing amount of satisfaction from their work when they feel in charge of it, see they are getting better at it, and perceive the overall purpose in it.

Focusing on process will make the product better in the long-run

School is about more than teaching us specific information, such as when the Declaration of Independence was signed or what a predicate nominative is. It does more than teach us specific skills, such as how to write in cursive or simplify radical expressions. A good education teaches us how to learn.

Knowing how to learn means that we can expand our knowledge and skills for the rest of our lives, not just during our years of formal schooling. As I've mentioned, strategies like cramming can boost test scores in the short term. But information that's "learned" this way is quickly forgotten and must be relearned for cumulative exams. When we focus on the processes of prioritizing tasks and studying ahead of time in many different ways, our children's grades will improve. But more importantly, their ability to learn will improve.

DEVELOP A GROWTH MINDSET

Focusing on the process is a powerful way to help your children grow, but it won't mean much if we retain an unhealthy understanding of academic ability and achievement. Dr. Carol Dweck of Stanford University conducted groundbreaking research on how we think about intelligence and how that mindset affects our performance.

Dweck divides the ways of thinking about intelligence, talent, and ability into two categories: the "fixed mindset" and the "growth mindset." Individuals with the fixed mindset view their intelligence as an immutable part of their identity, like height or eye color. Growth mindset individuals believe that they can become smarter by exercising their brains the way they can grow stronger by exercising their muscles.

Many parents unintentionally reinforce a fixed mindset in the way that they praise their kids. Dweck's initial research studied the effect of praise on children's willingness to accept challenges. Below is an excerpt from my book *Homework Made Simple* where I write about Dweck's findings and share her responses to my interview questions:

> *Praise is a powerful tool, especially when it comes to homework. Research shows that by simply praising effort rather than intelligence, kids will develop greater motivation to keep trying, even when the going gets tough.*
>
> *Dr. Carol Dweck conducted a landmark study on the effects of praise on 400 fifth graders. One at a time, the children were given a fairly easy, non-verbal IQ test. After randomly dividing the children, some were praised for their intelligence ("You*

must be smart at this") and the others were praised for their effort ("You must have worked really hard").

Later in the testing session, the same children were given a choice of tests. They were told that they could choose a more difficult test than the first one, but that they'd learn a lot more from this type of test, or they could choose an easy test, very similar to the first one. Results indicated that the type of praise they received after the initial test significantly affected their decisions on repeat testing. Ninety percent of the students commended for the effort chose the more difficult task. The majority of those praised for intelligence chose the easy test. The "smart" kids took the easy way out. Why did Dr. Dweck think this happened? She stated, "When we praise children for their intelligence, we tell them that this is the name of the game: Look smart and don't risk making mistakes."

Research shows that by simply praising effort rather than intelligence, kids will develop greater motivation to keep trying, even when the going gets tough.

In another round of testing, none of the students had a choice. Each child was administered an assessment [that was] two years ahead of their grade level, and every child failed. However, their approach to the test varied significantly. Those who were praised of their effort "got very involved, willing to try every solution to the puzzles." The students praised for their intelligence gave up easily and looked "miserable." Finally, after having induced failure, Dweck gave another test similar to the very first easy one. Remarkably, the children who had been praised for effort improved on their first score by about 30 percent, but those who were told they were smart did worse. Their scores declined by 20 percent.

Dr. Dweck stated, "Simply emphasizing effort gives a child a variable they can control. They come to see themselves as in control of their own success." This affects homework, because kids who feel in control are more likely to exert greater effort to get their work done well. They are more likely to persevere in the face of difficulty.

Psychologist (and former educator) Angela Duckworth echoes Dweck's findings in her book *Grit: The Power of Passion and Perseverance*, proposing that the ability to learn quickly and easily (typically measured in IQ) is just one component of success in both school and life.[49] She studied children and adults in all kinds of challenging situations and found that the quality that best predicted success was something she called "grit."

Duckworth defines grit as the combination of passion and perseverance for very long-term goals. It's not just the ability to work hard; it's the ability to work hard over a long period of time. She found that grit was more important than IQ, talent, family income, and even school quality in determining long term success.

Other studies bear this out as well. A study of high school and college performance conducted by the University of Oregon found that a willingness to work hard over a long period of time was more important than high school performance and test scores in determining success in college.[50] In short, the character we build in our children over the years matters much more than their grades.

REMEMBER THE BIG PICTURE

If you had to choose between your child getting straight A's on every report card and becoming independent and resilient, which would you choose? Of course, we want both. But sometimes focusing too much on grades can cause us to shortchange our children's opportunities to develop into self-sufficient adults. We keep intervening in their lives—keeping track of their work and talking to their teachers—because we are so afraid of them failing on their own. But all these little interventions add up, and sometimes even the highest academic achievers end up missing out on some crucial life-skills.

Sometimes focusing too much on grades can cause us to shortchange our children's opportunities to develop into self-sufficient adults.

As the Dean of Freshmen at Stanford University for over a decade, Julie Lythcott-Haims encountered thousands of the nation's highest achieving young adults and noticed something disturbing. These incredibly accomplished students were heavily dependent on their parents to help them select classes, choose a career path, and even navigate basic social interactions. They worked extremely hard, but they had little idea why they were working so hard. In her book, *How to Raise an Adult: Break Free from the Overparenting Trap and Prepare Your Kid for Success*, Lythcott-Haims observes that these kids appeared content to let their parents run their entire lives and make all their decisions well into their twenties.

None of those Stanford parents likely set out to keep their children dependent on them into adulthood, but it's very easy for all of us to do when we focus on grades at the exclusion of all other life-skills. Yet when we look past traditional academic achievement to our children's overall growth and development, wonderful things can happen. Fights turn into discussions, while sources of stress and anxiety transform into challenges that produce strength and resilience. Instead of feeling like they are constantly falling short of our expectations and desires, our kids feel inspired to push themselves to newer and better goals.

Different parents have different dreams for their children. But all of us want our kids to become mature, independent adults. We want them to be good citizens who will be able to take care of themselves and their families and contribute to their communities. And we want to have healthy relationships with our children that will last into adulthood. School and grades are just a small part of these goals, and our families will be healthier and happier when we keep them in perspective.

A QUICK RECAP

- Some conflict over schoolwork is inevitable, but it can and should be minimized.

- Possible sources of conflict include children's shorter time horizons, differing priorities, and limited maturity, as well as parents' anxiety about the future, vague or unreasonable standards, and communication choices.

- Focusing on the process of learning rather than on grades will help build stronger character and ultimately improve performance.

- Emphasizing growth over intelligence by praising effort rather than results will help children accept more challenges and become more confident in their ability to learn.

- Grades are just a small part of life, and good grades are not essential to long-term success.

Bonus Chapter 1

The Elementary School Procrastinator

Elementary school is a wonderful time for kids to explore their world and lay the foundation for strong academic performance in the future. It's also a great opportunity to build planning and organizational skills that will serve them well in the years to come. But most importantly, it is a time for kids to just be kids. Because even the most academically-motivated elementary school students should spend plenty of time playing outside and making friends.

Research shows that homework in elementary school does not contribute to short-term or long-term academic achievement.[51] In fact, many parents and educators observe that excessive homework in elementary school may cause unnecessary stress and discourage creativity and curiosity in students. Fortunately, many schools are realizing this, and assigning less homework to elementary school students than they once did. Others are eliminating it altogether.

Even without much homework, some kids will begin displaying tendencies toward disorganization and lack of planning, which can lead to procrastination later on. Elementary school offers a chance to work on these skills proactively, before they become an academic issue. Parents can do this by creating healthy routines that encourage the development of the helpful habits we covered in Chapter 2, keeping in mind that the overall goal of elementary school is to move children toward independence.

THE ELEMENTARY SCHOOL CHALLENGE: MOVING TOWARD INDEPENDENCE

One of the biggest concerns my tutors and I hear from parents of elementary schoolers is their uncertainty about how much they should be helping their children. They want to be involved and give their kids all the support they need, but they don't want to hinder them from becoming self-sufficient.

During the preschool years, kids are dependent on their parents for almost everything. They learn to tie their own shoes and wash their own hands, but they need Mom and Dad to keep track of their possessions and their schedules. The big challenge for elementary school parents is balancing their children's need for help with these tasks with their need to learn to handle them on their own.

At the beginning of kindergarten, you may pack your child's lunch and backpack for him and either drive him to school or walk him to the bus stop. You will also have his entire schedule organized and ensure he knows what he has going on each day of the week. But as he grows, you want to begin to teach him how to do these things for himself.

Of course, each child develops the ability to manage these tasks at a different pace, so your children may not all be ready for the same responsibilities at exactly the same ages. But the overall goal can be that by the end of elementary school, kids are organizing their own possessions and beginning to organize their own time. By fourth or fifth grade, it is reasonable to expect your children to be responsible enough to know what their homework is, to complete it, and to turn it in without any help from you.

The overall goal can be that by the end of elementary school, kids are organizing their own possessions and beginning to organize their own time.

MAKING THE MOST OF ELEMENTARY SCHOOL

The first day of elementary school is a huge milestone for any child, and every family approaches it differently. While there's plenty of preparation that lies outside the scope of this book, here are a few steps I recommend:

1. **Attend the orientation and talk to your child about what to expect.** You will also want to anticipate any anxieties she may have about her teacher, what she will wear, where she will sit, and all the other new experiences she will have.

2. **Start preparing for each new school year in the last weeks of summer.** Of course, you will buy all the required school supplies, as well as any new clothes and everything needed

for breakfasts and lunches. But go ahead and let your children get involved in the planning. They should organize and label their own supplies and can even plan out what to have for breakfast and lunch each day. This helps them learn to think ahead.

3. **Take at least a week in August to gradually move bedtime and wake-time earlier.** The first day of school can also be a shock to children's bodies after the leisurely pace of summer, so this process will help them adjust after months of staying up late and sleeping in. It prevents kids from beginning the school year sleep-deprived and makes for a much smoother transition.

As I mentioned, elementary school is also the perfect opportunity to develop routines that will serve your kids well in the later grades. Some of these cornerstone routines include:

- **Build the after-school homework habit.** If your children have any homework at all, you may want to get them in the habit of coming home from school, taking a short break and then getting it done. The sooner they learn to complete tasks earlier in the afternoon, the less likely they are to procrastinate in the future when the workload gets heavier.

- **But also encourage outside play.** The exception to the after-school homework rule would be during the winter months in areas where kids will have very limited time outside because of the cold and dark. If your child's only chance to play outside is right after school, by all means let her play while she can. Kids need fresh air and exercise and the chance to have unstructured fun, especially after spending hours in a classroom. This is just as important as any academic task, especially in the early years.

- **Avoid television and electronics until later in the evening.** Even if your kids have plenty of free time after school, encourage outside play, board games, coloring, crafts, and reading for pleasure. This way, when they get more homework in middle and high school, they'll already be used to electronics-free afternoons, and they won't feel like television and video games are being "taken away" from them.

- **Get assignments and the backpack organized the night before.** As your children move through elementary school, teach them to put completed assignments in the homework folder, put the folder in the backpack, and put the backpack in the appropriate spot/Launching Pad for the morning. This gives them great practice for the years to come.

- **Start to use a calendar.** Elementary school is also a wonderful time to show your kids how to use a calendar. You might want to buy a large calendar and keep all the family activities on it. Take the time each week to talk to your kids about what's coming up for everyone. This is especially helpful since younger children often have to come along for their siblings' activities.

GETTING PAST ELEMENTARY SCHOOL PROCRASTINATION

Besides building healthy routines, the biggest key to getting past elementary school procrastination is using positive communication to build good habits for independence in the future. Remember to use powerful questions like:

- What are your priorities today?
- What's one thing you can do to make sure you remember everything for school tomorrow?
- Going forward, what's one thing you might do differently? (This question is very helpful when they make a mistake or face a disappointing outcome.)

These questions help to activate your children's executive functions, rather than just telling them what to do. If you suspect any problems like ADHD or anxiety, this is a great time to get them evaluated by a professional so you can begin helpful interventions.

Remember, colleges won't ask to see your children's elementary school report cards, so don't worry about them too much. Focus on building habits, skills, and character qualities that will lay a strong foundation for their future.

Focus on building habits, skills, and character qualities that will lay a strong foundation for their future.

Bonus Chapter 2

The Middle School Procrastinator

"I've never run into a person who yearns for their middle school days," observed Jeff Kinney, author of the wildly successful *Diary of a Wimpy Kid* books. Not every kid will have as tough a time with the transition to middle school as Kinney's protagonist, Greg Heffley, but most will identify with at least some of his struggles. Even the most confident kid can be a little intimidated by the changing social dynamics and increased workload, not to mention the onset of puberty.

My tutors and I see a lot of new middle schoolers in our tutoring center, so if your student is struggling to adjust, you're definitely not alone. But despite its challenges, middle school can be a great time to discover our children's strengths, strengthen their weaknesses, and set the stage for success in high school and beyond.

THE MIDDLE SCHOOL CHALLENGE: SO MANY TEACHERS!

At the beginning of elementary school, your children most likely had one teacher who taught them all their major subjects. That teacher probably had clear expectations for how he or she wanted assignments completed and a predictable routine for collecting all their work. Kids only had to remember where one classroom was, and they probably had the same desk the entire year!

Later in elementary school, they may have had other teachers for various subjects, but they still had a single homeroom teacher. This teacher would monitor their progress, provide a sense of continuity, and ensure that nothing major slipped through the cracks.

Middle school is totally different. Students are expected to be independent and responsible for getting themselves to class, figuring out what their assignments are, and turning them in on time. What's more, they now have seven different teachers, a reality that presents all sorts of new challenges:

- **Different classrooms.** Most middle schoolers will need to walk to seven different classrooms throughout the school day. The school building itself is usually much larger than their elementary school, which can be a little intimidating. Now, not only will they have to figure out how to get to each of their classes before the bell rings, but also how to exchange books at their locker and how to fit in a trip to the bathroom now and then.

- **Different systems of giving assignments and reporting grades.** Having seven different teachers presents more

Students are expected to be independent and responsible for getting themselves to class, figuring out what their assignments are, and turning them in on time.

than just the practical challenge of getting to class. It means seven different textbooks and seven different sets of expectations. Maybe three teachers use the school's homework portal to post homework assignments, two use Google Classroom, and two write everything on the board. They will also have different ways they want homework turned in. One may have a basket by the door, another may walk around and collect it, while yet another may expect it to be uploaded to the portal at home. All this can feel very overwhelming to an eleven-year-old!

- **Block scheduling.** Another big change in some middle schools is block scheduling, the system where students only attend half their classes for twice the length of time each day. In theory, this means that kids have an extra afternoon to get homework done, since each class meets only every other day. But often this system leads to kids starting their assignments at the last minute anyway, or maybe forgetting about them altogether.

All these challenges require a new level of—yes, you guessed it—organizational skills! The only problem is, as kids enter puberty, hormones stimulate the limbic system—which is the emotional center of the brain—while their prefrontal cortex is still not completely developed.[52] This means that emotions can often override executive functions, making organizational tasks feel even more overwhelming than they would otherwise.

But more than any of these logistical challenges, most middle schoolers just want to make friends and fit in. They don't want to do anything that will make them appear different or draw unnecessary attention to themselves. Sometimes this even includes pulling out a notebook and copying down the homework assignment!

HOW TO PREPARE FOR MIDDLE SCHOOL

As you begin to prepare your children for middle school, keep in mind that anything that was an issue for them in elementary school will probably continue to be a challenge. For example, if they struggled with keeping track of their possessions in sixth grade, this is unlikely to magically get better in seventh grade. On the other hand, some subjects that used to be easy for them may become more difficult. It's very common for kids who were math whizzes with arithmetic and fractions to struggle a little in pre-algebra.

The good news is that most of these problems are related to the *transition* to middle school. Once students make the adjustment, they will most likely do just fine. Here are a few ways to make the transition to middle school a little easier:

1. **Attend the middle school open house with your child.**
   Even if you've been to open houses with your older children

and have heard everything before, this event gives your child an important opportunity to take a look at the new building and get a feel for what the next couple of years will be like. It will also enable you to meet all your child's teachers and find out important information.

2. **Find out how assignments will be given and how grades will be reported.** As we mentioned, these procedures could be different in each of your child's seven classes, so it's very important to write them down and ask questions if something seems unclear. Can students take a picture of the assignment with their phones? Are grades reported daily or weekly? Will the school send out an interim report card on a regular basis? You will want the answers to all these questions and more before the school year begins.

3. **Find out each teacher's re-take policy.** Most middle school teachers will allow students to re-take tests if they get below a certain grade. Some will allow only one re-take per quarter, while others may allow more. Be sure to find out the details from each of your child's teachers.

4. **Find out how students can get extra help.** Most teachers make themselves available during lunch, after school, or during a free period if students need extra help. Some ask children to sign up for an appointment while others allow students to just walk in. Find out each teacher's preference, so your child will know how to get extra help in each subject when needed.

5. **Have your child practice walking to all his classes three times.** This gives him a chance to get very familiar with his schedule and will reduce the anxiety associated with the first day of class.

6. **Have your child practice opening her locker three times.** If you supply your own combination lock, she can also practice at home.

7. **Have your child reach out to friends about class and lunch schedules.** Another source of anxiety for kids in middle school is wondering who they will sit with at lunch. Most schools have different lunch periods, but students can reach out to one another before the year begins and figure out who has which lunch period and with whom they can sit. Many students also like to find out if they have classes with any of their friends.

GETTING PAST MIDDLE SCHOOL PROCRASTINATION

Middle school means more homework and more opportunities to procrastinate. But applying some of the key principles in this book can go a long way toward overcoming procrastination:

- **Keep up the afterschool homework habit.** Remember, the goal is to automate the homework routine. Most middle schoolers still need parents to help them stick to a time and place for homework and studying. Be sure to have your middle schooler block off time in her schedule for this, either on paper, in her phone, or both. Encourage her to write down her quizzes, tests, and larger projects on a calendar or planner, or to enter them into an electronic organizer. Continue to have her work on homework in the optimal locations mentioned in Chapter 2, and avoid having her do homework in her room whenever possible.

Middle school kids are old enough to have a little more freedom, and sometimes they may prefer to stay after school and get their work done in the media center or school library. This can help some kids focus, and many enjoy not having as much work to do when they get home.

- **Set up a weekly appointment with your child to go over her grades.** Be sure to look at grades with your child regularly in middle school, even if you've never had problems before. Some parents may be inclined not to worry about grades until they see the first interim. But middle school is an adjustment for every student, and you don't want to be caught by surprise a few weeks in, when your child may already be way behind.

  Other parents may be tempted to check grades behind the child's back on a daily basis. But often this can lead to the parent getting upset and confronting the child as soon as she comes home. This is rarely productive and can weaken the parent-child relationship unnecessarily. Having a regular weekly appointment to check grades gives your child enough accountability, but also enables her to be independent. If, after the first quarter, your child is doing well, you can check in with them less frequently.

- **Investigate strengths and weaknesses.** Middle school is a great time for kids to experiment with different study methods to discover the ones that work better for them. When they do well on a test or assignment, ask them what they did to prepare that worked. And if they do poorly, try to figure out what might work better in the future. Remember, the purpose of these questions is to help children learn about themselves so they can build on their strengths and improve their weaknesses.

- **Investigate interests and passions.** Middle school is a great time to help your children discover subjects and activities that interest them, that preferably do not involve phones, television, or video games. In addition to academic subjects, these can be sports, music, hobbies, or other pursuits that enrich their lives and enable them to grow and make good friends. Remember that it is much easier for kids to focus on things that interest them, so helping them figure out their passions can help them improve their focusing skills as well.

- **Monitor work for completion, not quality.** Generally speaking, I recommend that parents of middle schoolers ensure their kids are completing their work and turning it in, while leaving the quality of the work to the teacher. Don't worry about checking to make sure all the math problems are done correctly or that their grammar and spelling are perfect in their essays. The teacher may expect mistakes that he or she will go over in class as part of the lesson. The goal in middle school is not only to provide oversight and accountability for your student, but also to enable him to grow toward even greater academic independence.

Middle school is a wild time for little boys and girls to transition into the teen years. Even the sweetest kids may give their parents a hard time now and then. But with the right preparation and strong routines, your child can thrive in middle school and beyond.

Bonus Chapter 3

The High School Procrastinator

If there's one thing I've noticed about high schools in my time as an educator, it's that no two are alike. The culture, classes, learning environment, and even class size vary widely, even between two public schools close to one another in the same county. The same is true (even more so) of the students who attend those schools. Many high schoolers will excel at academics. Others take an interest in athletics, art, or music. And a small handful of high school kids seem to excel at just about everything they do. Most parents, on the other hand, share the same goals across the board: to raise happy, healthy teenagers who are able to successfully navigate the college application process and grow into mature, productive adults.

Just like with middle school, the transition to high school can be a little tricky to manage. Middle school got students used to changing classes and dealing with lots of different teachers. But in high school, most college-bound students are placed in honors, Advanced Placement, or International Baccalaureate classes. Some teens have the raw ability to succeed in these courses, but may not feel ready for the increased workload or the fact that most teachers won't allow as many retakes as in middle school. Students who grew accustomed to doing assignments at the last minute, re-taking tests when they did poorly, or correcting work for partial credit may be in for a rude awakening in ninth grade!

In short, students who coasted by on natural ability in middle school may not be able to get the same results in high school with similar effort. In fact, it's not uncommon for some strong middle school students to be overconfident heading into their first couple of high school tests and then get demoralized when they receive lower grades than ones to which they're accustomed. Add to that the fact that these grades actually count on that all-important high school transcript that colleges will see, and the pressure is much greater on both parents and teens than it has ever been before.

THE BIG HIGH SCHOOL CHALLENGE: TIME MANAGEMENT

My tutors and I have found that the biggest challenge high school students face is managing their time effectively. High school is a time to transition from the carefree days of childhood to the responsibilities of adulthood. Students often have part-time jobs, earn their own money, open their own bank accounts, and learn to drive. They have greater freedom of movement and control over their own time than they ever did in the past.

But most high school students also have a growing number of obligations to balance in their schedules. Not only do they have school, but they may also have multiple activities that require large time commitments. Teens are often excited to join sports and clubs, and these are certainly a healthy and important part of the high school experience. But most high school sports teams practice five or six days a week, while participation in band, orchestra, a high school play or many other school clubs and activities can also be very time-consuming. Add a part-time job or volunteer obligations, and their days get pretty packed.

And then of course they have to study. As we've covered already, it's very important that your high schooler is well-matched to the classes he's taking. Taking classes that are too easy will not effectively prepare him for college, while taking classes that are too difficult will set him up for struggle. To complicate matters more, many high schools utilize block scheduling, resulting in longer class periods that meet less frequently. Students will also have many more projects, term papers, and cumulative exams than they faced in middle school. All this means that time management is a bigger challenge and more important than ever. Without the watchful eyes of Mom and Dad, high school students have to learn to block off time in their own schedules to take care of their responsibilities and then stick to that schedule on their own.

On top of all these new responsibilities, puberty is in full swing in high school. Not only can teens be moody, but they are also developing their own personalities, preferences, and opinions. These changes will affect all their relationships, including those with their teachers. It's not uncommon for a high school student to insist that a particular teacher just doesn't like him or that he just can't deal with the way that teacher presents material.

At the same time that they are figuring out who they are as individuals, most high school students remain very concerned about fitting in with their peers. They can spend a lot of time and energy on their appearance or other superficial things that strike adults as very silly. But all this is a normal part of growing up. Parents can guide and encourage them through this process, but high school is something teens will eventually have to figure out own their own.

HOW TO PREPARE FOR HIGH SCHOOL

The transition to high school is definitely challenging, but it's also an opportunity to help your son or daughter grow. Taking a few simple steps can not only make the transition more bearable, but set up your teen for success:

1. **Attend the open house.** Just like in middle school, this event is very important to help your teen get a feel for what the school building is like and where all his classes will be.

2. **Practice walking the schedule three times.** Many high schools are huge, with thousands of students and multiple floors of classrooms. Students need to practice getting to all their classes as quickly as possible. Another trend my tutors and I have noticed in our tutoring center is that high schoolers are not using lockers the way they once did. This may be due to the distance they must walk to get to class in such a short period time, as well as to the move away from heavy textbooks to online texts and worksheets. But it also means that keeping the backpack organized is more important than ever.

3. **Find out each teacher's policies and procedures.** Just like with middle school, all of your teen's teachers may have

Parents can guide and encourage them through this process, but high school is something teens will eventually have to figure out own their own.

different ways to give assignments and report grades. They may have different policies about re-taking tests as well as getting extra or partial credit. Be sure to find out all these details for each of your student's classes.

4. **Find out all the options for getting extra help.** Because high school classes typically move at a quicker pace than students are used to, it's very important that they know how to get extra help when they need it. Most high schools have multiple tutoring options, from the teachers themselves to older honor society students or other volunteers.

5. **Reach out to friends ahead of the school year.** Just like with middle school, knowing ahead of time who is in your teen's classes and lunch period can ease some of her anxiety about that first day.

6. **Encourage students to reflect on middle school successes and challenges.** The teen years are a time of increasing self-awareness, including a growing understanding of which techniques and strategies work best for them academically. The better teens grasp their own strengths and weaknesses, the more success they will have and the more they can improve.

7. **Consider proactive organizational coaching.** When students have managed well in middle school but have also shown signs of disorganization or executive function weaknesses, some parents prefer to get organizational coaching at the beginning of high school, rather than wait for a problem to show up. They find that their teens are more receptive to an outside adult who can help them think through the new challenges they will face and organize their time effectively. Some parents find that students can manage well on their own after a few weeks, while others elect to keep the coaching longer.

GETTING PAST HIGH SCHOOL PROCRASTINATION

Almost every high schooler will procrastinate at some point. The goal is for students to experience the consequences, learn from their mistakes, and do better next time. In fact, students who have never experienced any sort of failure before college have no way of knowing how to handle the inevitable setbacks they will face in adulthood. It's far better for them get practice in high school when they still have the support of their parents nearby.

The following are some of the habits that will help students develop the skills to stay on-task and rebound from mistakes on their own:

- **Students should start assignments the day they are received, regardless of the due date.** It's very easy to ignore a long-term assignment the day you get it. But just writing a thesis statement for a term paper, reviewing half a chapter of information for a cumulative biology test, or working on a couple of calculus problems will give your student a better sense of what a long-term assignment will require. This helps her plan her time more effectively and realistically and makes the assignment easier to pick back up in the days to come.

- **Students should make a plan and stick to it.** With all the time management challenges we mentioned above, it is absolutely crucial that high school students learn to plan out their days and weeks carefully. They can start by looking at the blocks of time that are taken up by school, work, sports, and other obligations. Then they will need to figure out where to find enough time to complete their homework and study for their tests. They may also need to factor in time to prepare for the SAT or ACT, while seniors need to allow time for filling out college applications. Parents can help by talking to their teens Sunday nights about the week ahead. Those powerful questions—*What do you have coming up? What might get in the way of your plans?*—still really help get high schoolers thinking and planning.

- **Students should ask for help right away.** As I've mentioned, because high school content moves quickly—especially in AP and IB classes—students should not delay asking for help when they don't understand a concept or are uncertain about the specifics of an assignment. The longer they wait, the further behind they will get.

- **Parents should go over grades with the student weekly, at least at first.** Just like with middle school, you want to monitor academic progress closely at the beginning to ensure your student is able to adjust successfully. If everything is going well after the first quarter, you can consider backing off and checking less frequently. The ultimate goal is for your teen to monitor her own progress out of her own internal motivation. At the same time, you don't want to your student to get too far behind without you knowing it.

The students who are able to succeed in college are those who have had an opportunity to practice being independent in high school.

As you might have noticed, unlike the recommendations I've provided for elementary and middle schoolers, these guidelines fall almost entirely on your student, not you the parent. This is because it is largely up to your teen, not you, whether or not he succeeds in high school. As discussed in Chapter 8, too much interference from parents can actually lead to worse long-term outcomes than allowing high schoolers to figure some things out on their own.

According to psychologist Madeline Levine, the most important goal in childhood and adolescence is developing a strong sense of self or identity.[53] To do this, high schoolers must learn to be independent, which is impossible if their parents are constantly intervening on their behalf. Instead, parents should support their teens' attempts to solve their own problems and forge their own paths forward.

In my experience, the students who are able to succeed in college are those who have had an opportunity to practice being independent in high school. This may allow them to make a few mistakes, but it will also enable them to develop a much greater sense of confidence in their ability to take care of themselves. And that—more than perfect grades—is far more important to success in college and beyond.

Bonus Chapter 4

The College Procrastinator

Is college an indispensable component of success in life or a waste of time and money? The answer depends almost entirely on what students do when they get there.

College is still far from a universal adult experience in America, but it is much more common than it used to be. In 1940, when the U.S. Census first collected data on educational attainment, just 4.6 percent of Americans had a four-year college degree. Today, over a third of American adults do,[54] and two thirds of high school seniors enroll in some sort of college the following year.[55]

But just getting admitted to college is no guarantee students will graduate. According to the National Student Clearinghouse, just 55 percent of students who entered college in the fall of 2008 were able to graduate within six years.[56] While some students drop out because of financial problems or family emergencies, many are simply unprepared for the academic demands and responsibilities.

As parents, there is nothing we can do to guarantee our students will have the perfect college experience. In fact, every one of them will face challenges and setbacks of some kind. But we can give them the tools they need to anticipate these challenges, face them effectively, and make the right choices moving forward.

THE BIG COLLEGE CHALLENGE: SO MUCH FREE TIME!

I asked my oldest son—who attended a private high school and (at this writing) is a sophomore in college—which aspects of his high school experience best prepared him for college. He mentioned that the volume and type of writing his high school teachers had demanded of him—which had annoyed him a little at the time—was a great advantage in his college courses. Some of his peers, who were very bright and capable, had lacked that kind of preparation and struggled with college-level writing as a result.

But he also mentioned something that surprised me a bit. He said that working part time on the weekends had also been tremendously helpful. In fact, he said if he had it all to do over again, he would have worked during the week as well. His job had almost nothing to do with the academic demands of college. Instead, it gave him the opportunity to budget his money and manage his time more effectively.

The time management challenge in college can come as a shock to some students. Suddenly, instead of 35 hours of class a week, they only have around 15. Unless they are student athletes or part of ROTC, the rest of their time is their own. They can join clubs and other activities, but all those meetings are optional. In fact, most professors don't even take attendance, so students don't "have" to go to class. And the truth is, many 18-year-olds are not mature enough to handle this much freedom.

The time management challenge in college can come as a shock to some students.

For most new college students, it is extremely tempting to fill those "free" hours with sleeping in, socializing, and checking out the parties that seem to be going on every night. They are supposed to be there to learn, but they face countless new distractions and almost no accountability.

On the other hand, some students at highly selective colleges have the opposite problem. They may do almost nothing but go to class and study, neglecting their physical and emotional health. Unfortunately, there has been a spike in mental illnesses like anxiety and depression among college students recently, especially at elite institutions.[57]

Compared to most high schools, college classes can seem like an extreme form of block scheduling. Most meet only two or three times a week, and professors typically don't assign graded homework. Yet students may need to complete hundreds of pages of reading (or dozens of complex practice problems) just to understand what the professor is talking about in the lecture. If they fall behind, it can be extremely difficult—if not impossible—to catch back up.

Instead of being spread across dozens of tests, quizzes, and assignments, students' final grades in most classes will be based on just a few evaluations: often a midterm, a paper or project, and a final exam. Diligent high schoolers probably spend a week studying for a cumulative exam, but in competitive colleges, exams require multiple weeks of daily preparation to perform successfully. Students need to have mastered the skill of putting these exams and assignments on their calendars and breaking them down into daily and weekly tasks. If they do poorly on just one of these tests or assignments, their final grade is unlikely to recover.

While some colleges inflate grades by moving the class average up when too many students do poorly, others actually deflate grades, allowing only a small number of students to obtain A's or even B's. Add to all this the fact that most colleges require that students maintain at least a 2.0 GPA to remain enrolled, and a student who goes to a few too many parties first semester may quickly find himself on academic probation.

Professors' expectations of the student role in learning are often very different in college as well. Unlike high school teachers, most college professors do not give out study guides that explain everything that will be on the exam. They expect students to listen carefully to lectures, complete all the assigned reading, and determine for themselves what information is most important.

Writing expectations are different too. The "five-paragraph essay" format most students learn in high school (that is also encouraged on the SAT and ACT) is completely different from the type of writing most college professors require.[58] Many students who got A's on all their high school papers are shocked when the same effort produces a C or below in college.

But the challenges of college go beyond academics. Students are usually living away from home for the first time, which means they must keep themselves fed, do their own laundry, get themselves to the doctor when they don't feel well, and so on.

They need to budget their money and must manage any inter-personal conflicts with roommates or hall-mates without their parents' help. And while these challenges relate to students' independence rather than academic preparation, they are just as likely as academic problems to cause students to drop out.

PREPARING FOR COLLEGE SUCCESS

Many high school students may be drawn to particular colleges for all kinds of reasons that have nothing to do with how successful they can be at the school or after they graduate. In addition to prestige, they may be interested in a school because of its football or basketball team, its dorms and facilities, its meal plan, or even its climate. It's up to parents to help their students look past these superficial qualities to the actual education and training that they will receive at the school and how that fits in with their overall goals in life.

My tutors and I do not typically see college students in our tutoring center, but we worked with one particular student "Casey," who was enrolled in a state university a couple of hours away. Casey had struggled with organizational skills in high school, but she had been admitted to her first-choice college and was very excited to attend. She was determined to work harder than ever and do well.

Unfortunately, once she got to school, Casey was completely unable to live up to her own expectations. It wasn't that she lacked the desire to excel or the willingness to work hard. In fact, she would spend all afternoon in the library, determined to study. Yet even after several hours at a desk, she would hardly have gotten anything done. She simply didn't have a realistic

understanding of her own ability to focus and study productively. Casey was placed on academic probation and eventually
had to leave the school.

Fortunately, Casey was able to transfer to a university that
was a much better fit for her capabilities. Our tutors began offering her organizational coaching over the phone. Knowing that
attention naturally wanes after forty or fifty minutes, we helped
her break down her study tasks into twenty- to thirty-minute
blocks. Between tasks, she could take a short break and then
switch subjects just as discussed in Chapter 6. She also began
studying in a few different locations—instead of always at the
library—and switching between subjects more frequently. After
feeling as though she had failed herself and her family, Casey
finally began to experience a turnaround in her academics.

Casey's story is not at all uncommon. Many new college
students struggle, and some drop out or transfer. There is no
foolproof way to prevent this from happening, but there are
some steps you can take to help your son or daughter make the
right college choice the first time around:

- **Visit a wide variety of schools.** Give your teen a chance
  to tour many different kinds of schools, large and small,
  rural and urban, more and less competitive, to help her get
  a feel for what's out there. Many colleges and universities even offer high school seniors the opportunity to visit
  overnight or take a class for dual high school and college
  credit during the summer. These visits give them a chance
  to talk to college students extensively and get a better
  sense of what life is really like at that particular school.

Many new college students struggle, and some drop out or transfer.

- **Inquire about the support available at each school.** Before your teen selects a school, find out what kind of academic support they offer. Although college students are assigned an academic advisor, they are expected to take the initiative to get help when they need it. This can involve seeing their professor during office hours, making an appointment with the teaching assistant, or signing up for peer tutoring, depending on what the school makes available.

- **Have your student reflect on what's working for him in high school.** By this age, it is very important for students to develop an awareness of how they study best and how hard they are willing and able to work. They should know which distractions tempt them the most, and how to overcome those temptations. If they are unable to make themselves focus during high school, they are unlikely to learn right away in college, when almost all accountability is removed.

- **Help your teen select a college that is a good fit.** Casey belonged in college; she just needed to find the right college for her. Many students are tempted to attend the highest-ranked school to which they're admitted. Yet, according to the National Center for Public Policy and Education, over 60 percent of college freshman are not academically prepared for college level work, despite being admitted.[59] And a 2013 study published in the *Journal of Labor Economics* found that a significant number of students are mismatched with their colleges, meaning their abilities do not fit well with the academic demands of the school.[60]

Teens mature as they get older, but they don't become entirely different people. The better your student's abilities are matched to the demands of his college, the better his chance of success. You want him to be sufficiently challenged, of course, but not overwhelmed the way Casey was. My tutors and I have seen many, many students blossom and grow at smaller or less-selective schools, leading to tremendous success after graduation. Remember that where they go to school is not nearly as important as what they do when they get there.

CONCLUSION

I asked my son what advice he would offer rising college students to help them succeed. He responded that they must know their own goals and hold themselves accountable to reach them. I couldn't agree more. College students should not be working just to please Mom and Dad anymore. They should be working to get the most out of their college opportunity for their own benefit.

College can be a wonderful time for young adults if they select a school that is a good match for their abilities and aspirations. Students who struggled with organizational skills during the grade school years can absolutely find success in college, but not by waiting for things to magically improve. They should anticipate the challenges of the college transition and arrive with strategies to navigate them successfully.

Notes

1 Andrea Cooper, "Stall Tactics: Helping Young Procrastinators," *Parenting* (retrieved September 2017 from https://www.parenting.com/article/stall-tactics-helping-young-procrastinators).

2 "Eighty-seven Percent of High School and College Students are Self-Proclaimed Procrastinators" *Study Mode* (May 17, 2014).

3 Sarah Spinks, "Adolescent Brains are a Work in Progress," *PBS Frontline* (January 31, 2002).

4 Harvard University Center on the Developing Child, retrieved from https://developingchild.harvard.edu/science/key-concepts/executive-function/

5 As I mentioned in the introduction, this book is written primarily to address the struggles with procrastination faced by children and their families dealing with some form of executive function weaknesses. I am not a psychiatrist or a medical doctor, so I do not address the use of medication to control or manage ADHD or any other condition. I also do not directly address the needs of children suffering from trauma, abuse or saddled with more severe learning disabilities.

6 Christopher Bergland, "New Paradigm of Thought Demystifies Cognitive Flexibility," *Psychology Today* (September 7, 2015).

7 Shirley S. Wang "To Stop Procrastinating, Start by Understanding the Emotions Involved," *Wall Street Journal* (August 31, 2015).

8 "Study Looks at Impact of ADHD on Homework," *Yellin Center for Mind, Brain, and Education* (November 30, 2016).

9 "How Long Does it Take to Form a New Habit?" *University College of London News* (August 4, 2009).

10 According to the National Sleep Foundation, school age children need 9 to 11 hours of sleep each night, while teenagers need 8 to 10. Children who do not get enough sleep may be sleepy in school, but they may also be hyperactive, excessively talkative, moody, combative and prone to emotional outbursts. Lack of sufficient sleep has been shown to exacerbate ADHD symptoms, so it is even more vital that parents of children with these struggles help them get enough high quality sleep. See Nan Norins, "Lack of Sleep Shown to Worsen ADHD Symptoms in Children," *Children's Hospital of Wisconsin* (November 19, 2013).

11 As Harvard Professor Anne Fishnel explained in the *Washington Post*, what you eat for dinner doesn't matter nearly as much as making the time to sit down together, free from other distractions, and share a meal. She explains that children learn even more words at the dinner table than they do from being read to by the parents, boosting their vocabulary. Regular family dinners are also highly correlated with high test scores in high school, as well as lower risk of *"smoking, binge drinking, marijuana use, violence, school problems, eating disorders and sexual activity."* See Anne Fishnel "The Most Important Thing You Can Do With Your Kids? Eat Dinner with Them," *Washington Post* (January 12, 2015).

12 Although video game apologists have touted their ability to boost mood and reaction time, they have also been shown to trigger the fight or flight response: raising the heartrate, firing up the nervous system and draining resources away from systems the body considers non-essential. See Victory Dunkley, "This is Your Child's Brain on Video Games," *Psychology Today* (September 25, 2016).

13 Larry Rosen, Alexandra Samuel, "Conquering Digital Distraction," *Harvard Business Review* (June 2015).

14 A 2006 meta-study conducted by Duke University Professor Harris Cooper confirms that about 10 minutes of homework per grade level per day produces optimal results. See "Duke Study: Homework Helps Students Succeed in School, As Long as Their Isn't Too Much," *Duke Today* (March 7, 2006).

15 Michael Rugg, Mark A. W. Andrews, "How Does Background Noise Affect Our Concentration?" *Scientific American* (January 1, 2010).

16 L. Edwards and P. Torcellini, "A Literature Review of the Effects of Natural Light on Building Occupants," *National Renewable Energy Laboratory* (July 2002).

17 Benedict Carey, "Forget What You Know about Good Study Habits," *New York Times* (September 7, 2010).

18 "College Students Struggle with Organizational Skills," *RP Newswire* (November 2006).

19 Karsten Strauss, "These are the Skills Bosses Say New College Grads Do Not Have," *Forbes* (May 17, 2016).

20 Anthony P. Carnevale and Nicole Smith, "Workplace Basics: The Skills Employees Need and Employers Want," *Human Resource Development International* (November 18, 2013).

21 Shira Springer, "Why is it so Hard to Stop Buying More Stuff?" *Boston Globe* (May 18, 2017).

22 The same goes for notetaking. *"Writing by hand is slower and more cumbersome than typing, and students cannot possibly write down every word*

in a lecture. Instead, they listen, digest, and summarize so that they can succinctly capture the essence of the information. Thus, taking notes by hand forces the brain to engage in some heavy 'mental lifting,' and these efforts foster comprehension and retention. By contrast, when typing students can easily produce a written record of the lecture without processing its meaning, as faster typing speeds allow students to transcribe a lecture word for word without devoting much thought to the content." See Cindy May, "A Learning Secret: Don't Takes Notes with a Laptop," *Scientific American* (June 3, 2014).

23 J.M. Langberg, J.N. Epstein, A.J. Graham, "Organizational Skills Interventions in the Treatment of ADHD," *Expert Review of Neurotherapeutics* (October 8, 2008).

24 Nobel Prize winner Daniel Kahneman and Amos Tversky first proposed this concept in their 1979 paper *The Planning Fallacy.*

25 These distinctions have recently come under fire, mostly because of the methodology in the studies used to support them. *"Unfortunately, the answer is no, according to a major new report published this month in Psychological Science in the Public Interest, a journal of the Association for Psychological Science. The report, authored by a team of eminent researchers in the psychology of learning—Hal Pashler (University of San Diego), Mark McDaniel (Washington University in St. Louis), Doug Rohrer (University of South Florida), and Robert Bjork (University of California, Los Angeles)—reviews the existing literature on learning styles and finds that although numerous studies have purported to show the existence of different kinds of learners (such as "auditory learners" and "visual learners"), those studies have not used the type of randomized research designs that would make their findings credible."* However, if you find a different method of presenting concepts to your child works better, by all means use it! See "Learning Styles Debunked: There is No Evidence Supporting Auditory and Visual Learning, Psychologists Say," *Association for Psychological Science* (December 16, 2009).

26 See Eric Hanushek, "The Economic Value of Higher Teacher Quality," *Urban Institute, National Center for Analysis of Longitudinal Data in Education Research*, Working Paper 56, December 2010. Published version can be found at *Economics of Education Review,* volume 30, Issue 3, June 2011, pp. 466–479.

27 Writing in the New York Times, professor and author Daniel T. Willingham discusses the degree to which preexisting knowledge influences the development of skills such as reading comprehension. *"In one experiment, third graders—some identified by a reading test as good readers, some as poor—were asked to read a passage about soccer. The poor readers who knew a lot about soccer were three times as likely to make accurate inferences about the passage as the good readers who didn't know much about the game."* The same strong association between previous knowledge and high reading scores held true for passages about science, civics, geography and the arts.

See Daniel T. Willingham, "How to Get Your Mind to Read," *New York Times* (November 25, 2017).

28   Chris Weller, "There's an Epidemic of Grade Inflation and Unearned A's in American High Schools," *Business Insider* (July 18, 2017).

29   Sarah D. Sparks, "Research Finds Students Short on Study Savvy," *Education Week* (June 5, 2012).

30   Peter C. Brown, Mark A. McDaniel and Henry L. Roediger III, "Make it Stick: The Science of Successful Learning," *Harvard University Press* (2014).

31   Ibid.

32   Ibid.

33   Peter Brown, Henry Roediger, and Mark McDaniel, *Make it Stick: The Science of Successful Learning*, Belknap Press, 2014.

34   Deborah Halber, "Sleep Helps Build Long Term Memories," *MIT News* (June 24, 2009).

35   Kessler RC, Chiu WT, Demler O, Merikangas KR, Walters EE. Prevalence, severity, and comorbidity of 12-month DSM-IV disorders in the National Comorbidity Survey Replication. *Arch Gen Psychiatry.* 2005 Jun;62(6):612-27

36   Merikangas, K. R., He, J., Burstein, M. E., Swendsen, J., Avenevoli, S., Case, B., . . . Olfson, M. (2011). Service Utilization for Lifetime Mental Disorders in U.S. Adolescents: Results of the National Comorbidity Survey Adolescent Supplement (NCS-A). Journal of the American Academy of Child and Adolescent Psychiatry, 50(1), 32–45. doi:10.1016/j.jaac.2010.10.006

37   Maria Zimmitti is the founder and president of Georgetown Psychology of Georgetown, McClean and Bethesda and Cathi Cohen is the founder and director of InStep PC of Fairfax.

38   Bita Ajilchi, Vahid Nejati, "Executive Functions in Children with Anxiety, Depression, and Stress Symptoms," *Basic and Clinical Neuroscience* (2017 May–Jun; 8(3): 223–232.)

39   David Ludden, "How to Overcome Math Anxiety," *Psychology Today* (March 4, 2017).

40   Melina Delkic, "Lack of Sleep May Cause Depression, Anxiety," *Newsweek* (September 7, 2017).

41   "Blue Light Has a Dark Side," *Harvard Health Letter* (December 30, 2017).

42   Leah Shafer "Social Media and Teen Anxiety," *Harvard Graduate School of Education* (December 15, 2017).

43   According to the Anxiety and Depression Association of America, anxiety-based school refusal now affects between 2 and 5 percent of school. See Samantha Raphelson, "Educators Employ Strategies to Help Kids with Anxiety Return to School," *NPR* (October 16, 2017).

44 William Harms, "Writing About Worries Eases Anxiety and Improves Test Performance," *University of Chicago News* (January 13, 2011).

45 Madeline Levine, *The Price of Privilege*, Harper Collins, 2006.

46 Elaine Mcardle, "Ed. Extra: Earn to Learn?" *Harvard Ed. Magazine*, (Winter 2010).

47 Amanda Ripley, "Time Magazine—Should Kids Be Bribed to do Well in School?" *Education Innovation Laboratory at Harvard University* (April 12, 2010).

48 Ross Brenneman, "Gallup Student Poll Finds Engagement in School Dropping by Grade Level," *Education Week* (March 22, 2016).

49 Angela Duckworth, "Grit: The Power of Passion and Perseverance," Scribner, 2016.

50 "The 2012 Report Card on the Ethics of American Youth," *Josephson Institute Center for Youth Ethics.*

51 Ann K. Dolin, "Homework Made Simple: Tips, Tools, and Solutions to Stress-Free Homework," *Advantage Books* (September 2010). Used with permission.

52 Annie Murphy Paul, "Does High School Determine the Rest of Your Life?" *Time* (November 18, 2013).

53 Madeline Levine, *The Price of Privilege*, Harper Collins, 2006.

54 Kate Reilly, "Is Homework Good for Kids? Here's What the Research Says," *Time* (August 30, 2016).

55 Marian Arain, Maliha Haque, Lina Johal, Puja Mathur, Wynand Nel, Afsha Rais, Ranbir Sandhu, and Sushil Sharma, "Maturation and the Adolescent Brain," *Neuropsychiatric Disease and Treatment* (April 3, 2013).

56 Reid Wilson, "Census: More Americans Have College Degrees than Ever Before," *The Hill* (April 3, 2017).

57 Floyd Norris, "Fewer US Graduates Opt for College after High School," *New York Times* (April 25, 2014).

58 "Completing College: A National View of Student Attainment Rates— Fall 2008 Cohort," *National Student Clearinghouse Research Center* (November 2014).

59 "Beyond the Rhetoric: Improving College Readiness Through Coherent State Policy," *National Center for Public Policy and Higher Education* (2010).

60 Eleanor Wiske Dillon and Jeffrey Andrew Smith, "The Determinants of Mismatch Between Student and College," *Journal of Labor Economics* (August 2013).

About the Author

Ann K. Dolin, M.Ed. is a former public school teacher in Fairfax County, Virginia, author of *Homework Made Simple— Tips, Tools and Solutions for Stress-Free Homework* and *A Guide to Private Schools: The Washington DC, Northern Virginia and Maryland Edition,* and the founder of Educational Connections Tutoring. What once started as an hour of tutoring at a kitchen table has grown to a nationally recognized tutoring and educational coaching company which allows Ann to help countless kids overcome academic obstacles and improve their confidence and grades.

Made in the USA
Middletown, DE
04 July 2019